LETTING GO OF TOXIC RELATIONSHIPS

Break Free from Unhealthy Patterns, Recover from Emotional Wounds, Create New Boundaries, and Rebuild Your Self Worth

KAREN CREHAN

Copyright © 2024 Karen Crehan. All rights reserved.

The content within this book may not be reproduced, duplicated or transmitted without direct written permission from the author or the publisher.

Under no circumstances will any blame or legal responsibility be held against the publisher, or author, for any damages, reparation, or monetary loss due to the information contained within this book. Either directly or indirectly. You are responsible for your own choices, actions, and results.

Legal Notice:

This book is copyright protected. This book is only for personal use. You cannot amend, distribute, sell, use, quote or paraphrase any part, of the content within this book, without the consent of the author or publisher.

Disclaimer Notice:

Please note the information contained within this document is for educational and entertainment purposes only. All effort has been expended to present accurate, up-to-date, and reliable, complete information. No warranties of any kind are declared or implied. Readers acknowledge that the author is not engaging in the rendering of legal, financial, medical or professional advice. The content within this book has been derived from various sources. Please consult a licensed professional before attempting any techniques outlined in this book.

By reading this document, the reader agrees that under no circumstances is the author responsible for any losses, direct or indirect, which are incurred as a result of the use of the information contained within this document, including, but not limited to, — errors, omissions, or inaccuracies.

CONTENTS

Part One
THE MANY ASPECTS OF TOXIC RELATIONSHIPS

Introduction	9
1. Toxic Relationships and the Harm They Create	13
2. Unraveling the Causes and Breaking Free	39

Part Two
TAKING CONTROL BACK

3. Setting Boundaries for Toxic Relationships	53
4. Separating from a Toxic Relationship	63
5. Dealing With the Aftermath	79

Part Three
REGAINING YOUR WORTH

6. Rewriting Your Story-Begin Healing the Emotional Wounds	93
7. Self-Compassion and Deeper Healing	109
8. Trusting Yourself and Others	129

Part Four
EMBRACING LIFE

9. Reclaiming Your Essence and Believing in Yourself	143
10. Begin Thriving, Creating Your Future	155
11. Moving Forward with Your Life	167
Conclusion	179
References	185

I would like to express my gratitude to everyone who has helped me along my journey of growth throughout the years. To my childhood friends who stood by me, my family who have opened my eyes, to my high school friend whose life ended too soon from a toxic relationship, to the people I've met in the most synchronistic ways. To my friends and colleagues who saw more potential in me than I could see in myself and helped push me along on my soul's evolution. The encouragement, love and support I have received is a testament to this book. I hope by reading this, it helps you on your journey.

Part One
THE MANY ASPECTS OF TOXIC RELATIONSHIPS

INTRODUCTION

The journey from being involved in a toxic relationship to rediscovering your inner worth is possible and vital to your well-being. It begins with the understanding that a relationship you are in has a harmful, negative impact on you. You must find the courage to say that you no longer want to live this way and realize that this relationship is slowly eating away at your self-esteem.

Toxic relationships wear down your boundaries. They can make you feel incapable or uncertain of yourself. Restoring boundaries is the first step to creating a change. I was in a relationship like this. It felt like an exhausting battle until I took control back. This book is a testament to the possibility of transformation. It is the beacon of hope for those who feel trapped and gives you the tools you need to shift the dynamics.

My healing journey began over a decade ago as I embraced my role as an energy healer and Reiki master. I witnessed the incredible strength and resilience of the human spirit as I assisted other individuals with their desire to break free from the binds of toxic relationships. But truthfully, it was the heart-wrenching experience of seeing my daughter entangled in such a relationship that truly opened my eyes. It mirrored my struggles, making me see that these toxic patterns I was fighting to heal in others were also part of my life.

This profound realization sparked a journey of deep reflection and healing. Witnessing both the turmoil and the inner strength that my daughter developed from leaving this toxic relationship broadened my understanding and my compassion even more. As an empath, I feel the pain of those struggling in similar relationships, and this book is my commitment to guiding you toward freedom and healing from this manipulation.

Almost everyone has been in some toxic relationship. They occur at different levels, some subtle and some outright destructive. These relationships are marked by manipulation and control and create emotional turmoil. At the core of these relationships are individuals, often narcissists, who are battling their own inner demons, perhaps unaware of the toxicity they spread. They are acting subconsciously from their inner, hurt child, trying to grasp control. They deny any wrongdoing. They reject change and react with hostility when challenged.

In doing this, they subconsciously believe that this provides them with the safety and security they so desperately need and crave. They may play on your sympathy and act like a hurt puppy. They may often tell you to calm down, diminishing your concerns about a valid situation. The truth

INTRODUCTION

is, no matter how much support or love you give them, they will not change unless they do their inner healing work.

There are also the more devious relationships, those who deliberately manipulate situations so they can feel powerful and in control. These relationships span beyond the romantic, affecting multiple aspects of social life. It can be your boss, a parent, a teacher, a friend, a roommate, a coworker, or a family member. Understanding the nuances of these dynamics, from subtle manipulations to overtly harmful behaviors, is crucial to identifying them.

Part of the healing process is letting yourself feel and express your emotions of anger, frustration, or sadness. Allow yourself to feel this, acknowledge it, and then be willing and determined to walk away from this manipulation. When you have a clear understanding of toxic relationships, you are empowered to recognize the behavior and stop it from progressing any further.

The heart of this book is to guide you to understand and separate yourself from toxic relationships and embark on a journey of healing and self-discovery. Transforming pain into strength and reclaiming your self-worth begins here. With the words of wisdom from Rumi and other visionaries, you are invited to reflect, feel uplifted, move on, and grow.

Each chapter is designed to guide you through every step of your journey, from understanding the dynamics to leaving a toxic relationship and through the healing process. It is an inclusive guide, acknowledging that toxic relationships do not discriminate. The insights within these pages offer solace and strategies to anyone ready to step away from this toxicity.

As you turn each page, absorb the information and let the statements and affirmations resonate deeply, nurturing your spirit. Engage with the exercises provided; each is a step towards regaining a sense of empowerment and self-worth. I speak to you not just as an author but as a fellow traveler on this path of healing. As you journey through this, you begin to feel love and compassion towards yourself and learn to trust your instincts as you navigate the complexities of relationships. Know that you are seen, understood, and, most importantly, capable of breaking free.

I invite you to take that first courageous step toward healing and empowerment. This journey may challenge you, but it promises a transformation that will renew your essence, guiding you to a place of self-compassion and continued growth. Let's embark on this path with open hearts, unwavering hope, and determination.

TOXIC RELATIONSHIPS AND THE HARM THEY CREATE

Never wish them pain. That's not who you are. If they caused you pain, they must have pain inside. Wish them healing. That's what they need.

— NAJWA ZEBIAN

Understanding the dynamics of manipulation in a relationship becomes crucial for self-preservation and your mental health. In a perfect world, your partner is willing to examine the interplay of the relationship and be willing to make the effort towards improvement. This is the beginning step of a healthy relationship.

If the individual refuses to acknowledge that there is a problem, becomes defensive, makes a dismissive comment suggesting that your feelings are unimportant, cuts you off mid-sentence, or talks over you, then realize that this is a toxic relationship. A narcissist personality has no genuine interest in what you are doing or feeling. Everything revolves around what they want and what is convenient for them.

This manipulation affects you emotionally and can eventually manifest in your physical body, making you sick. Victims of this abuse can experience adrenal spikes, a response to stress, which can lead to exhaustion and other related health issues.

Research shows that prolonged emotional abuse can alter the part of the brain that regulates emotions and self-perception.

Staying in a relationship like this will eventually undermine you and devalue who you are, even to yourself. It is vital that you recognize this and work on changing the dynamics before you become incapacitated with an illness or injury. It is time to begin walking away from this unhealthy dynamic and tend to yourself first.

This chapter delves into seven common forms of toxic behavior in relationships, explaining how each works, the harmful effects, and strategies for distancing yourself from the damaging effects and, ultimately, reclaiming healthy control of your life.

LOVE BOMBING: OVERWHELM, CONTROL, AND CONFUSION

At the beginning of a new relationship, the affection and attention can feel like your hopes and dreams have been answered. Within this dream can lie a potential nightmare known as 'love bombing.' This toxic behavior is an overwhelming bombardment of love that is inappropriate for the length of the relationship. During the high phase, the manipulator uses extreme affection and desire to create a sense of euphoria. This can often be mistaken for passion or a deep emotional connection, but it is designed to hook you emotionally and make you crave their affection and approval. The intensity overloads the recipient to the point where their ability to see clearly becomes clouded.

Love bombing is also the strategic showering of expensive gifts and flattery to gain control or influence over the other person. The love bomber puts their intended target on a pedestal and can go into debt with extravagant spending to earn the affection of their victim. Love bombers use gifts to manipulate and control their target by creating a sense of indebtedness or obligation. This ultimately backfires as the bills roll in, and then the love bomber subconsciously blames the recipient and begins to withdraw their affection and admiration from them.

This skewed perception of love is like an emotional rollercoaster, when the love bomber often withdraws affection to exert control, leaving their target feeling desperate for the next 'love fix.' The extreme contrast between the warmth and the coldness is upsetting, making the individual yearn for the high again. This low phase is often abrupt without any apparent cause, leaving the recipient confused and anxious and wondering what they did to cause this. This withdrawal of affection is not for giving space or the natural ebb and flow of intimacy; it is a subtle act of power and control. Love bombers use manipulation tactics to control their target's emotions and behaviors.

Recognizing the Signs and Patterns

The difference between sincere love and manipulative overtures requires an awareness that something doesn't seem right or is too good to be true. Genuine affection grows steadily and respects boundaries. It feels secure and comforting. Conversely, love bombing feels like a relentless pursuit, marked by extravagant gestures that may seem out of place. Love bombers make you feel special and may say, "There is no one else like you," or "No one understands me like you do." This tactic is very manipulative, using excessive affection and praise as a means of control and subtle domination.

Love bombing often disregards personal boundaries, pushing for more intimacy and commitment than is comfortable. The relationship moves quickly, racing ahead and often making grand plans.

Identifying this behavior in your relationship is critical to breaking free from its grip. The pattern repeats itself, becoming a predictable rhythm of ups and downs that slowly erodes your sense of self and your ability to trust your feelings. Here are some signs that you are caught in this cycle:

- **Observation**: You start to notice a pattern where periods of affection are predictably followed by phases of withdrawal or neglect. This repeating pattern raises red flags. It suggests the individual may be controlling things instead of expressing true feelings.

- **Walking on eggshells**: You find yourself constantly trying to navigate the relationship carefully, avoiding anything that might trigger a shift to the low phase. This constant state of alertness is exhausting and not conducive to a healthy, supportive partnership.
- **Blame and confusion**: During the low phases, you may be blamed for the change in dynamics, leading to self-doubt and confusion. This can include guilt-tripping, emotional blackmail, or playing on your insecurities. The manipulator may suggest that your actions, or lack of them, cause the shift and that you are to blame. This distortion is designed to keep you second-guessing your behavior.

Tips to help identify and protect oneself from this manipulative tactic:

- **Intensity vs. intimacy**: Notice if the relationship is moving unnaturally fast. Genuine intimacy takes time to develop and does not rely on grand gestures.
- **Put on a pedestal**: Love bombers often idealize their target and overlook flaws or imperfections. They may project their fantasies onto the target, creating an unrealistic image of the perfect partner.
- **Listen to your gut feelings**: If something feels off, it probably is. Trust your gut if the affection you are receiving feels overwhelming or unearned.
- **Seek outside perspectives**: Sometimes, being in the midst of a situation can cloud your judgment. Consulting with trusted friends or family about the relationship can provide clarity.

- **Appearances can be deceiving**: The love bomber may appear quite charming and friendly to those in your social circle. You may be the only one who sees and experiences what it's like to be in a closer relationship with this person. Keep a written record to validate your experience of what transpires between you.
- **Maintain independence**: Keep up with your hobbies, interests, and social circle. Love bombers often seek to isolate and monopolize your time and attention, so maintaining independence is vital.
- **Set and enforce boundaries**: Communicate your boundaries early on. A genuine partner will respect them, while a love bomber may push back or disregard them.

The Harm it Creates

The impact of love bombing on the psyche is tremendous. Initially, the high—filled with overwhelming praise, attention, and promises of happiness—makes you feel cherished and valued. The highs are so rewarding that they can reinforce your tolerance for the lows. It creates a dependency loop, where the victim craves the highs of the love bomber's affection, mistaking it for loving intimacy or friendship.

Love bombing significantly impacts your emotional well-being. This constant uncertainty and emotional whiplash can contribute to anxiety and depression. The unpredictable oscillation between the extremes of highs and lows can leave you feeling unworthy, unlovable, and inadequate and wondering if you are responsible and deserve this treatment.

Over time, this can erode your self-esteem, making it harder to leave the relationship or seek healthier dynamics.

The stress of navigating the cycle can also lead to physical symptoms, such as insomnia, fatigue, and changes in appetite. Staying alert and aware of this behavior can free you from the confusion and control that love bombing brings. Realizing the dynamics of this empowers you to recognize manipulative affection, differentiate it from genuine love, and protect yourself from this unhealthy relationship.

Understanding the early signs of love bombing can shield you from becoming entangled in its snare. Recognizing this cycle is crucial because while the highs can be intoxicating, the price paid for the lows is too high. This pattern is a trap that keeps you tethered to a cycle of manipulation and emotional turmoil. This manipulative tactic keeps you off-balance and emotionally invested. Breaking free from this dynamic requires acknowledging the pattern, understanding its impact on your well-being, and resolving to navigate away from this cycle towards healthier, more stable grounds.

GASLIGHTING: THE MANIPULATION AND HARMFUL EFFECTS

At its core, gaslighting is an intentionally harmful form of emotional abuse. The perpetrator attempts to make the victim doubt their memories, perceptions, and even their sanity, using manipulative behaviors to undermine the victim's confidence in their own thoughts and feelings. The term originated from the 1938 stage play "Gas Light," where a husband manipulates small elements of the home environment to convince his wife that she is losing her mind.

This goes beyond spousal relationships. It can also be in parental and other relationships of authority.

Gaslighting is a deliberate tactic to destabilize and disorient the victim, making them question their reality. Unlike physical abuse that can leave visible scars, gaslighting wounds the psyche, creating a web of doubt that entraps the victim. It is a subtle yet powerful manipulation that can completely change a person without leaving any visible trace. The gas lighter will subtly shift blame by saying that they treat you a certain way because of your behavior.

A gas lighter employs various strategies to sow the seeds of doubt. These include blatant denial of events that have occurred, contradicting the victim's recollections, and lying about facts even when there's concrete evidence. If confronted with a specific behavior, the gas lighter may deny it ever happened or accuse the victim of making it up. When a person is subjected to this abuse, they are often manipulated to believe that their reactions and emotions are not valid or are exaggerated. The gas lighter will deflect attention away from their actions by saying that their victim is always overreacting or being paranoid.

The repercussions of this type of treatment are profound. Over time, the constant questioning of one's reality can lead to significant self-doubt and the erosion of self-esteem. The victim begins questioning their judgment and their sanity. Their sense of reality becomes increasingly tethered to the gas lighter's version of events. As the doubt creeps in, an unhealthy dependency develops, chaining the victim to the very source of their uncertainty.

Understanding gaslighting helps to recognize this form of emotional abuse and safeguard yourself from it. Recognizing this harmful behavior gives you the awareness to trust your perceptions and reclaim the truth of your experiences.

Breaking free from the gas lighter's grip can often be challenging, as gaslighting is designed to be invisible. Talk to someone you trust about your experiences for external validation and perspective to counter the lies and isolation imposed by the gas lighter. Keeping a written record of interactions can help clarify experiences the gas lighter manipulates. Record conversations on your cell phone as proof of the interactions.

Seek support from a therapist or support group to rebuild your self-esteem and develop coping strategies and assertiveness skills. Educating yourself about gaslighting and its effects will empower you to recognize the signs of manipulation and tactics. Realizing that you are not alone, that your experiences are valid, and that support is available can be highly transformative. Trusting your instincts and creating boundaries begins the journey of regaining self-trust and mental clarity.

GHOSTING

Ghosting is a form of toxic behavior in which a friend or romantic partner abruptly cuts off all communication without giving any explanation or warning. The expression comes from when an individual vanishes into thin air or disappears from your life. This can occur in various relationships where the person will stop responding to your text messages, emails or phone calls.

Early warning signs are that you are always texting first, your partner's responses are very brief, there is no effort or apologies for not responding at all, they often make excuses to break plans that you made together, or they blatantly ignore you even when you see that they are actively online.

Some individuals are not intentionally malicious. They realize that you have different opinions, and they don't want a confrontation or are afraid to hurt your feelings. They may be overwhelmed by some situations, or they might have a fear of commitment. Ask them if they're okay. However, realize that no response is a response. The effects of being ghosted can be deeply hurtful and damaging to the person being ignored. Some common effects are:

- **Feelings of rejection and abandonment**: Being ghosted can trigger feelings of rejection, abandonment, and unworthiness. The sudden disappearance of the other person without closure can leave the victim questioning what went wrong and doubting their self-worth.
- **Confusion and anxiety**: Not knowing why the other person disappeared can lead to confusion and anxiety. The lack of closure can leave the victim second-guessing their behavior and wondering if they could have done anything differently to prevent them from being ghosted. The individual can feel embarrassed and not want to tell friends about the perpetrator's sudden disappearance.
- **Loss of trust**: Ghosting can erode trust in future relationships. The experience may make the victim hesitant to open up to others or invest emotionally in

new relationships, fearing they will be abandoned again without warning.

In some cases, the toxic individual may intentionally manipulate the situation to continue the cycle of ghosting and control. This manipulation can take various forms, such as:

- **Intermittent reinforcement**: The manipulator may sporadically reappear or send mixed signals to keep you guessing and emotionally invested in the relationship. This is called soft ghosting or breadcrumbing, connecting just enough to string you along.
- **Gaslighting**: The perpetrator may deny or minimize their actions, making the victim question their perceptions and reality. They may blame the victim for the breakdown of the relationship or accuse them of overreacting.
- **False promises**: The person may make empty promises or express intentions of reconnecting in the future to string you along and maintain control over the relationship dynamics. Haunting or orbiting means they will occasionally make their presence known to you but will not actively reach out to you.
- **Manipulative tactics**: The abuser may use guilt, pity, or emotional manipulation as a power play to keep the intended target emotionally attached and vulnerable and willing to overlook their toxic behavior.

The victim needs to recognize these manipulation tactics and prioritize their emotional well-being by setting boundaries and distancing themselves from the toxic individual.

Finding closure after being ghosted can be challenging, but there are steps the person can take to help them move forward:

- **Acceptance**: Being ghosted hurts. Remember, you deserve to be treated with courtesy and respect. Accept that the other person has chosen to end the relationship in a cowardly and disrespectful manner. Try not to take it personally. Recognize that ghosting reflects the other person's shortcomings, not your own.
- **Focus on self-care**: Prioritize self-care and activities that bring you joy and fulfillment. Surround yourself with supportive friends and family who can provide comfort and reassurance during this difficult time.
- **Seek closure through reflection**: While you may never receive a satisfactory explanation from the manipulator, take some time to reflect on the relationship and any potential red flags or issues that may have contributed to its demise. Self-reflection helps you gain insight and closure on your terms.
- **Closure through communication**: If you feel comfortable, consider contacting the individual to express your feelings and seek closure. Let them know that ghosting hurts more than saying this relationship isn't working. Be prepared for the possibility that they may respond dismissively or not

at all. Remember that closure ultimately comes from within, and you cannot control the actions or responses of others.
- **Move forward**: Once you have processed your feelings and gained closure to the best of your ability, focus on moving forward with your life. Allow yourself to heal from the experience and remain open to new connections and experiences in the future. The best revenge for being ghosted is to keep living and thriving.

ISOLATION

In the myriad of toxic relationships, isolation is a silent predator. It is a tactic employed by manipulators to separate their victims from their network of support, making them more vulnerable, dependent, and easier to control. This isolation is not always overt. It can start subtly, masquerading as concern or love, making it harder to recognize until the web has been tightly woven around their victim.

The perpetrator might discourage you from spending time with others, suggesting that your friends or family do not have your best interests at heart. They may criticize your friends and family, planting seeds of doubt about their intentions. They may tell you that your good friend is nothing but trouble or a little wild. These comments can lead to tension and distance you from your friends who know you best.

Isolation tactics can also include controlling who you see, when you see them, and even how you communicate with them. It is like being placed in an invisible cage, where the bars are made of guilt, manipulation, and supposed concern for your well-being.

The end goal of isolation is complete dependency. The victim becomes increasingly reliant on their partner as they are cut off from the people who know them and can offer perspective and support. It creates an environment where leaving feels impossible because of the disconnection from the world. It's a cruel illusion of care, where the manipulator positions themselves as the only one who truly understands or cares while systematically stripping away their victim's independence.

An example of this tactic is to imagine moving to a new city for love, where the only person you know is your partner. It sounds like an adventure, but it can also be a calculated move to isolate you from your support system. If this was not a mutual decision, be aware. Moving to an unfamiliar place is a significant step that can lead to dependency on your partner for social connections, emotional support, and even basic needs like transportation or financial support.

Creating dependency is a multifaceted strategy. It's about ensuring that, over time, you rely on your partner for emotional support and your sense of identity and reality. This dependency can manifest in several ways, including controlling the finances so you do not have the means to leave. In extreme instances, they isolate you to the point where they become your only social contact, which can deepen the sense of dependency and make the outside world seem alien and intimidating.

Identifying the Subtle Forms

Not all forms of isolation are apparent. It is crucial to recognize the early warning signs before the isolation deepens.

- **Subtle discouragement**: Pay attention if your partner subtly discourages you from seeing your friends or family, perhaps by sulking or becoming uncharacteristically quiet when you mention them. You may be challenged and tested to see what you will put up with.
- **Overbooking**: The abuser attempts to fill up your schedule with activities just for the two of you, leaving no room for others.
- **Criticizing your support system**: Slow, consistent criticism of your friends and family can make you question those relationships and, over time, choose to distance yourself to avoid conflict.

Understanding these subtleties can be your first line of defense, helping you maintain your support network even in the face of manipulation.

Harmful Psychological Effects

In a healthy relationship, partners lean on each other but maintain their autonomy and connections outside the relationship. In a toxic one, the balance shifts drastically; your world gradually narrows until it consists only of your partner, making the thought of leaving or challenging the status quo feel insurmountable.

- **Loss of self-esteem**: Constantly being told, directly or indirectly, that you are incapable of managing without your partner wears down your belief in your abilities.
- **Impaired decision-making**: Over time, the chronic doubt sown by your partner can make you distrust your judgment, deferring more and more to their decisions.
- **Fear of independence**: The thought of being on your own can become filled with anxiety, reinforcing the belief that you are unable to cope without the relationship.

The impact of this dependency on your self-esteem and decision-making capabilities can be profound, eroding your confidence and making you second-guess every decision that does not align with your partner's wishes. Recognizing these signs is crucial. Awareness is the first step toward reclaiming your freedom, your connections, and, ultimately, your independence. As you navigate these challenges, remember that isolation thrives in silence. Breaking that silence by reaching out to trusted friends, family, or professionals can be the key to unlocking the cage.

JEALOUSY

Jealousy is a common human emotion, but it can sometimes take a dark turn, becoming a tool for control within relationships. Jealously is characterized by the fear of loss and a desire for exclusivity. While jealousy may sometimes be interpreted as a sign of possessiveness or protectiveness, it ultimately stems from insecurity, mistrust, and a lack of confidence in the individual.

When left unchecked, jealousy grows from a fleeting emotion into a constant presence, overshadowing the relationship with suspicion and distrust. This excessive monitoring is an attempt to control your behavior under the guise of care and protection. When left unchecked, it lays the groundwork for a toxic dynamic, where one partner's jealousy restricts the other's freedom. For example, the jealous individual may accuse you of deliberately attracting another person's attention or take offense when you talk to someone else. This partner might claim their jealousy is a sign of love, but it is a means of control.

Signs of an Unhealthy Jealousy and the Impact

Using jealousy as a pretense to demonstrate care can undermine trust in the relationship. It suggests that your partner does not trust you to make your own choices. This begins to erode the foundation of trust that is essential for a healthy relationship. Recognizing signs of control masked as concern is the first step toward addressing the imbalance. These signs may include:

- **Monitoring communications**: Checking phones, emails, or social media without consent, under the pretense of caring and having your best interest at heart.
- **Limiting social interactions**: Discouraging or outright forbidding you from seeing certain friends or family members, often labeling them as 'bad

influences' or claiming 'they're jealous' of your relationship.
- **Dictating choices**: Making decisions for you, from what you wear to how you spend your time, citing their 'better judgment' or 'just wanting the best' for you. When you express your dissatisfaction with something in the relationship with the hopes of improving it, they might respond with something like, "If you're not happy, you can leave and go home to your mother," knowing that this is something you don't want to do.
- **Inducing guilt**: Making you feel guilty for spending time away from them, even if it's for work, study, or personal growth, suggesting that your independence is taking you away from their love. You feel as if you must constantly reassure them of your devotion and faithfulness to them.

Unhealthy jealousy often leads to patterns of defensiveness, accusations, and emotional manipulation. You are left trying to prove your love and devotion to the perpetrator. Over time, this creates a communication breakdown in the relationship, making it difficult to address issues and resolve conflicts. Constant conflict and mistrust undermine the emotional bond between partners, leading to resentment and bitterness.

As the controlling behavior escalates, it chips away at your personal freedom and autonomy. This erosion is not always immediately noticeable. It often occurs gradually, making it challenging to recognize it until your choices, preferences, and even your movements start to feel like they are under constant scrutiny. This leaves little room for spontaneity or personal growth. The relationship becomes a confining space where your partner's insecurity dictates the terms of who you are and what you do, inhibiting your ability to express yourself freely with your appearance, hobbies, or opinions. As the jealousy escalates, you start fearing that your behavior will incite jealousy or anger. You become hesitant to go places or meet people independently, knowing it could lead to interrogations, accusations, or emotional blackmail. Your self-worth diminishes as your partner's perceptions and demands overshadow your needs.

Reclaiming Your Independence

Asserting your autonomy in the face of controlling behavior is not easy, but it is a critical step toward restoring balance and health in the relationship. Here are strategies to consider if there is the possibility that the person is willing to change:

- **Open communication**: Initiate a dialogue about your feelings and concerns. Be clear about the impact their behavior has on you and the relationship. It is essential to approach this conversation calmly and constructively, focusing on your feelings rather than assigning blame. If they are willing to acknowledge and take responsibility for their action, set firm boundaries. Do not take any excuses because this can be further manipulation.
- **Set clear boundaries**: Define what is acceptable and what isn't regarding your behavior and theirs. Boundaries are not ultimatums; they are guidelines that help maintain respect and autonomy within the relationship.

- **Professional guidance**: In some cases, couples counseling or individual therapy can be invaluable in navigating the complexities of jealousy and control. A professional can offer neutral, informed advice and strategies for coping and healing. If your partner refuses to do this, be aware they are unwilling to change.

Only you know what your partner is capable of doing. Jealousy can lead to rage. In extreme cases, unhealthy jealousy can escalate to emotional or physical abuse. The jealous individual may resort to tactics such as intimidation, threats, or violence in an attempt to control your behavior and maintain dominance in the relationship.

Ask yourself if your partner is willing to let you go. If you fear violence, seek outside help from a trusted family member or friend and ask if they can assist you in leaving this toxic relationship. If you have seen signs of aggressive behavior, protect yourself and have an exit strategy firmly in place. There are domestic abuse agencies that help in developing a safety plan to keep you from harm. Many of these agencies have 24-hour crisis hotlines staffed by trained advocates who provide immediate support and referrals to individuals in crisis. Your safety is your top priority.

FINANCIAL ABUSE

Financial manipulation is a form of control that strips away a person's economic independence and security, creating a dependency on the abuser. Financial abuse involves controlling a person's ability to use, acquire, and maintain financial resources. Victims of this form of abuse are often entirely dependent on their abuser for money, which significantly limits their ability to make choices that could allow them to escape the relationship. It is a tactic that traps the victim in an abusive relationship and erodes their self-confidence and ability to function independently in the world.

Financial abusers employ both overt and covert methods to exert control and dominance. They can withhold money by limiting access to bank accounts, providing an allowance, and controlling how and when money is spent. They will question purchases and demand receipts to monitor and control spending. They will resort to criticizing, mocking, or punishing the victim for any expenditure that they deem unnecessary. This punishment is not necessarily physical. It can be withholding affection, the cold shoulder, or silent treatment.

In a more extreme case, the abuser can sabotage employment by disrupting the victim's ability to work. The abuser may create emergencies that demand their partner to leave work or harass them in their workplace, or worse yet, inflict injuries that make it impossible to go to work. They can also create financial debt by taking out credit in the victim's name without their consent, often ruining their credit score and making financial independence a difficult dream to attain. Awareness of this financial abuse is crucial to prevent it from taking over your life. Signs include:

- **Lack of access to bank accounts**: Not knowing account passwords or being kept in the dark about financial matters.

- **Unexplained debts or credit issues**: You may discover debts you didn't know existed or find that your credit score has plummeted without cause.
- **Employment sabotage**: Noticing a pattern of crises or demands from your partner that negatively affect your work.
- **Feeling guilty for normal spending**: If buying necessities or the occasional treat for yourself creates anxiety over potential backlash, it is a red flag.

Escaping Financial Control

Breaking free from the grip of a financially abusive relationship requires resolve, planning, and support. Here are some suggestions to help you regain financial autonomy:

- **Have a financial safe space**: Open a bank account solely in your name, one your partner does not know about.
- **Create extra income**: Ask for additional work hours or get a second job. Even small, regular deposits can grow into a fund to help you gain independence.
- **Seek professional help**: Financial advisors, legal aid, and domestic abuse organizations can offer guidance and resources to help you navigate away from financial abuse.
- **Educate yourself**: Familiarize yourself with fundamental financial concepts and money management. Learn and understand the endless money drain from credit card debt. Do not spend beyond your means. Taking control of your finances builds your confidence in handling money.

- **Utilize resources**: Specific government agencies have been created to help you. Information is available online to guide you to the right places. Spend time researching to find the help you need and utilize it. Many communities have programs designed to assist victims of abuse, including financial abuse. These can range from shelters offering temporary housing to organizations providing financial grants or loans to help you get back on your feet.
- **Document everything**: Keep a record of all financial transactions, including any instances of abuse. This documentation can be crucial if legal proceedings are required or when seeking financial assistance.

Taking control over your finances is a crucial step toward breaking free from this abusive relationship. It is more than just money. It is reclaiming your independence, confidence, and ability to make choices that best serve you for your future.

CODEPENDENCY

Fear creates another form of an unhealthy relationship. Codependency emerges from an individual with unmet needs and emotional neglect and now has very low self-esteem and no boundaries. Individuals who suffer from codependency find solace in caretaking but at the expense of their well-being. They subconsciously seek validation and purpose by caring for their partner, who also struggles with constant insecurity.

Beneath the surface of this individual lies a fragile ego hungry for admiration and a sense of control. At the receiving end of the relationship is the narcissist who thrives on attention at the cost of their partner's emotional health. The codependent clings to hope, believing they can help change their partner and earn their love.

The codependent believes their worth lies in their ability to please others. They sacrifice their needs, boundaries, and desires to maintain the relationship. They feel guilty when they stand up for themselves. They become a people pleaser, and this role spans out to all aspects of their lives as they attempt to please everyone but themselves. Subconscious fears keep them trapped in this relationship. Fear of abandonment and loss keeps them caught in this cycle. Even as their emotional reserves are depleted, they constantly try to soothe their partner's insecurities.

The narcissist thrives off the codependent's devotion. They demand attention, admiration, and validation to fill their need to be appreciated. Their emotional requirements never end, and they manipulate their partner to fulfill them. It is very much a one-sided relationship. They blame their partner for any misgivings and point out the things that make them feel inferior. They rarely reciprocate emotional support, leaving the codependent feeling empty and unloved.

Breaking the Pattern

Breaking free from this toxic tango requires courage and self-awareness: Both partners must acknowledge their roles. The codependent must see their worth beyond caretaking and find a way to leave this controlling relationship. The enabler in the relationship must confront their need for external validation. The codependent must learn to say no, even if it means disappointing the partner and set and maintain boundaries to protect their emotional well-being.

When the manipulative partner refuses to acknowledge or admit to wrongdoing, regaining your independence is an absolute necessity that requires strength, determination, and willingness to leave a toxic relationship. Remember, asserting your autonomy is not an act of defiance but a declaration of self-respect, which is the foundation of any healthy relationship.

> *You were born with potential. You were born with goodness and trust. You were born with ideals and dreams. You were born with greatness. You were born with wings. You are not meant for crawling, so don't. You have wings. Learn to use them and fly.*
>
> — RUMI

UNRAVELING THE CAUSES AND BREAKING FREE

Do not be satisfied with stories that have come before you. Unfold your own myth.

— RUMI

Toxic relationships are not just confined to the areas of romance. They can emerge anywhere humans connect, from the neighbors to the family dining table, between lifelong friends, or within the work environment. It can be very subtle, but these dynamics are characterized by behavior patterns that make you feel guilty, unsympathetic, selfish, or lazy. This diminishes your sense of self-worth, invading your personal boundaries and instilling a pervasive sense of unease or insecurity. Recognizing these patterns outside the context of romantic engagements begins fostering healthier interactions across all areas of life.

Addressing toxicity in non-romantic contexts presents its own unique challenges. Emotional bonds and shared history within families can make confronting toxic behavior difficult. Power dynamics and fear of repercussions can hinder one's ability to speak out in professional business and work settings. Friendships, often overlooked as sources of potential harm, can also harbor unhealthy patterns that are hard to recognize due to mutual affection and the shared history involved.

EXAMINING THE MANY ASPECTS OF TOXIC RELATIONSHIPS

The signs of toxicity in non-romantic relationships mirror those in romantic ones: subtle criticism, lack of support, gaslighting, and an imbalance of power, to name a few. However, these signs manifest differently depending on the relationship. For example, a toxic friend might regularly belittle your achievements under the guise of "just joking," while a family member might manipulate you into meeting their needs, disregarding your boundaries. In the workplace, a colleague or superior might take credit for your work, undermining your contributions and professional growth.

Recognizing these patterns takes time. As you realize the negative impact, you gain the power to choose differently and to seek relationships that affirm your worth, and mutual growth. Reflect on the relationships in your life where boundaries might be lacking or disrespected, and consider if you often feel overextended or undervalued. Start a reflection journal. Document the patterns you have noticed in your relationships. Notice if there are similarities to the dynamics you observed or experienced in your childhood. Draw connections and create awareness without judgment.

Reflect on the significant relationships in your life and consider these questions:

- What patterns do you see?
- How do these patterns mirror the dynamics from your childhood?
- What qualities would you like to seek in relationships moving forward?

This awareness is key to understanding when the dynamics of our relationships were set early in life. Untangling past connections to present relationships provides a sense of clarity as to why something is happening. Early trauma and neglect play a significant role in guiding our choices in selecting a partner. It's not a conscious decision but something ingrained in us by those who raised us. If chaos and coldness were familiar in your environment, this might feel like home in adulthood. If you lived in a household where shouting matches were the norm, as an adult, subconsciously, you are drawn to these partners who express love and anger with the same intensity.

Making conscious choices is a powerful tool for breaking free from the invisible ties of past experiences.

The beliefs we were taught early on can still control our behavior now. For instance, if you grew up in a religious family where wedding vows are considered sacred and binding, it might influence you to stay in an unhealthy marriage. But remember, the vow, 'till death do us part,' is not about a physical death. It's about the metaphoric death of a harmful belief that held us captive. Recognizing this can empower you to make a different choice to break free from an unhealthy relationship.

There is also the mistaken notion that staying in a marriage is more stable for the children who are involved in this situation. You may think that your self-sacrifice is better than the harmful results of a divorce, but this harms both you and the children involved. Children are very aware. As much as you think that you try to shield them from unpleasantness, they will realize what is happening. They sense the disharmony. Staying in a relationship like this can begin another cycle of an unhealthy, toxic relationship for the next generation because they are watching and learning from your behavior.

As we explore how childhood shapes the emotional landscapes of our adult relationships, and by connecting the dots, we start to understand that toxic relationships begin subconsciously from what we experienced in our youth. Grasping this understanding allows for a significant shift, breaking the patterns and beginning the healing.

THE CYCLES OF REPETITION

Our upbringing will influence what we will endure in a relationship. Recognizing this repetition is like turning on a light in a room that has been dark for too long, revealing both the mess and the way out. Adult relationships are often scripted from our childhood roles that were experienced. It becomes what we know and what we are familiar with. If your parents' relationship modeled that alcoholism or some other kind of substance abuse was tolerable or acceptable, you may find yourself in a similar situation. If you had a caregiver who was emotionally distant, you might find yourself drawn to partners who are hard to connect with, mistaking the struggle for love.

Unresolved childhood conflicts tend to subconsciously influence our choices, pushing us towards those who mirror the unresolved issues of our past.

A person who felt overlooked as a child may gravitate towards partners who make grand gestures of affection but are emotionally unavailable. The neglected child, now an adult, constantly seeks the validation they craved in childhood. This behavior is an unconscious attempt to fix what was broken. With understanding, we can change this story, but without this awareness, it often leads to repeating the same painful cycles.

The Impact of Emotional Childhood Neglect

Parental gaslighting, a form of manipulation where a child's reality is invalidated or denied, leaves deep scars. It can manifest in parents dismissing feelings by saying, "You're just too sensitive," or distorting facts by claiming, "That never happened," and minimizing a child's experiences by stating, "It wasn't that bad."

The outcome is a child who grows into an adult constantly questioning their perceptions and memories and carrying a backpack of doubt into every relationship. Neglect can take many forms, and it is often hard to detect. It makes a deep impact like any visible injury. It silently undermines the core of self-esteem and wellness. It can be difficult to resolve until you are ready, willing, and able to accept the emotional abuse that you endured.

Neglect chips away at the foundation of self-esteem; each act of indifference is a blow to one's sense of value.

It begins a silent erosion of self. Emotional neglect, as damaging as any physical absence, leaves scars hidden beneath the surface, shaping perceptions of love and worthiness in harmful ways. Over time, this disregard can hollow out the core of self-esteem, leaving behind a shell of the person once vibrant with hope and self-assurance. Emotional neglect occurs when an individual's feelings are consistently ignored or invalidated. It is the nonresponsive silence after sharing your deepest fears or the absence of comfort during your darkest moments.

Physical neglect is the disregard for an individual's physical well-being and basic needs for health. Psychological neglect is dismissiveness and a lack of importance for one's needs. This indifference stunts one's personal development and silently sends the message that the individual's needs are unworthy of attention or care.

Recovering from the Gaslighting Cycle of Manipulation

Shattering the cycle of gaslighting begins with acknowledgment. Recognizing the signs within your family dynamics is painful but pivotal. Seeing the manipulation for what it is without sugar-coating it or brushing it under the carpet is a breakthrough towards healing it.

After this realization, critical thinking begins by questioning the narrative you have been fed and comparing it with your memories and experiences. This does require a conscious effort to rebuild from within. Resources, especially cognitive behavioral therapy, can be instrumental in untangling the web of confusion and guiding you to trust your perceptions again.

The path to healing from parental gaslighting is personal and can be complex. It involves relearning trust in your perceptions and rebuilding self-esteem eroded by years of manipulation. This journey includes:

- **Self-care**: With years of neglect, building love and compassion for yourself takes time, but it is the way to heal. Prioritize activities that make you feel good about yourself and reinforce your worth. This could be anything from hobbies that bring joy to routine self-care practices that nurture your body and mind.
- **Understanding**: When you start hearing a parent's voice in your head telling you of your so-called shortcomings, stop it immediately. Acknowledge that this is the original cause of your distress. Let these thoughts go, and know the words are untrue. They were created by another hurt individual. You are the one who is stopping this pattern of hurt.
- **Seeking support**: Whether through support groups or trusted friends, finding a space to speak about your experiences is crucial. You can feel seen and heard there, perhaps for the first time. You can find these groups either in person or online. It is a safe place where you can share your experiences with others who understand. Being able to speak this validates your emotions and gives you a new field of understanding.
- **Therapy**: Therapists specializing in family dynamics can be invaluable in helping you unravel and heal

from these patterns. They offer a safe space to explore your feelings, reframe your experiences, and develop strategies to rebuild your self-esteem.

Reversing the Negative Effects of Neglect

The path to healing is paved with gentle steps of self-recognition and care. Begin to mend your heart and soul:

- **Acknowledging your wounds**: The first step is to look at your experiences of neglect, acknowledging their impact without minimizing or dismissing your feelings.
- **Self-affirmation exercises**: Embrace affirmations that remind you of your worth, repeating them as a mantra until they become the bedrock of your belief system. Phrases like "My feelings matter," "I trust my memories and judgments," and "I am worthy of acknowledgment" are powerful affirmations. These should be said multiple times throughout the day. We will dive into this even more in chapter 9.
- **Cultivating self-compassion and self-love**: Practice speaking to yourself with the same tenderness you would offer to a loved one. Each word of kindness boosts your self-worth. Treat yourself as if you were your most cherished friend. Don't blame yourself for anything that you did or experienced because of a toxic relationship. Realize that in a certain aspect, in the beginning, you thought you were being supportive or helpful to them.

Detaching from the cycle of neglect involves recognizing its presence and choosing to step out of its shadow. Begin by focusing on this:

- **Make conscious choices**: Choose the people you allow into your life, selecting those who show care and respect for your needs.
- **Set boundaries**: They protect your emotional and physical well-being and communicate these boundaries clearly to others.
- **Practice self-care relentlessly**: Self-care is not selfish. Understand that as you do this, you affirm your worth and right to be nurtured.
- **Value yourself**: This will take some time. Accept this with no judgment. Be alert and attentive to any negative self-talk that creeps in, nipping in the bud and changing the words into something supportive.

Healing happens on different levels. Be patient with yourself. There will be days when old doubts will resurface. You may hit a speed bump thinking you have faced a painful memory, and now another layer has been revealed. Each step forward, no matter how small, is a piece of reclaiming your truth and voice. Peeling the layers of the onions will cause you to shed tears, but these are healing tears.

Acknowledge that the hurt took years to build and will take some time to heal. If you've ever weeded a garden, you know that sometimes when you pull a weed, part of it breaks off, stays in the ground, and will reappear. This is a metaphor to show you how sometimes you think you've gotten to the root of a problem, but it comes back up again. There often are more layers to be cleared, but it gets easier each time you do it. It is a continuous process.

Every time you make peace with a painful memory, you have let go of some heavy baggage, better understand who you are, and can be more compassionate to yourself.

> *Be kind to yourself, dear-to our innocent follies. Forget any sounds or touch you knew that did not help you to dance. You will come see that all evolves you.*
>
> — RUMI

THE INTERPLAY BETWEEN LOVE AND FEAR IN TOXIC RELATIONSHIPS

In the complexity of human emotions, love and fear often intertwine. These two powerful emotions play a significant role in shaping the dynamics of relationships, particularly those tinged with toxicity. Love can be masked by fear. For example, a partner's overprotectiveness may initially seem like a sign of love and concern. However, a closer look reveals it as a manifestation of their insecurities and fears, projected onto the relationship to maintain control and avoid facing their vulnerabilities.

At its best, love is a force that nurtures, supports, and uplifts, fostering a sense of security and mutual respect between partners.

Fear, however, can masquerade as love. When fear infiltrates this bond, it morphs love into a tool for manipulation and control. This often manifests in ways that can be mistakenly interpreted as care or concern. For instance, a partner's insistence on constant communication might be framed as love. Still, beneath the surface, it is a mechanism of control driven by fear, fear of abandonment, betrayal, or the unknown. Fear keeps us trapped and afraid to be alone.

These fear-based attachments develop when the foundation of a relationship is not mutual respect and love but a shared dread of loneliness, abandonment, or unworthiness. Begin by identifying behaviors and patterns in the relationship that are driven by fear. Reflect on moments when actions were taken "because of love" were, in reality, attempts to alleviate anxieties or control the partner. By becoming aware of this, you can see if fear keeps you in an unhealthy relationship.

These partnerships are often marked by a cycle of emotional highs and lows, with the fear of losing the relationship—no matter how unhealthy—keeping one tethered to it. Other clues of an unhealthy relationship include constant anxiety about its stability, staying in an unhappy relationship to avoid loneliness, and making excuses for a partner's negative behavior out of fear of confrontation or loss. You may even lie or make excuses to protect your partner because you view this as some misconstrued sense of loyalty.

Disentangling Love from Fear

Separating genuine affection from attachments rooted in fear is finding clarity in chaos. Acknowledging this pattern is crucial. This is the first step in choosing to break free from the chains of past fears, paving the way for healthier relationships that are chosen, not endured. It requires introspection and, often, a shift in perspective and seeing it from another point of view.

Gently challenge these fears by taking small steps outside your comfort zone, reinforcing your capability and resilience. When you acknowledge that fear has been a driving force in the relationship, this reveals the layers of insecurity, control, and dependency.

Fear is a silent predator preventing you from being truly happy.

As you realize fear's manipulation, you see that your desires and hopes are not being met. This fear-based mentality has allowed you to settle for less or be used for the other person's benefit. As you come to terms with this, you can slowly shift this dynamic, adjusting to change it or seeking a healthier relationship based on mutual respect and love.

Recovering from any unhealthy relationship involves both flexibility and strength, which are necessary to create resilience that can weather life's storms. Both people in the relationship must be willing to change. If not, draw from your past experiences to navigate towards your future goals. See challenges as opportunities for growth and view any obstacles as a method of strengthening your resilience.

As we explore breaking free from toxic relationships, the journey begins with leaving what no longer serves you and coming home to yourself. Crafting emotional independence is like standing in a storm and knowing you can shelter yourself from it.

The wound is the place where light enters you.

— RUMI

Part Two
TAKING CONTROL BACK

SETTING BOUNDARIES FOR TOXIC RELATIONSHIPS

Don't be afraid of your fears. They're not there to scare you. They're there to let you know something is worth it.

— RUMI

Imagine a vibrant garden full of lush plants and flowers. Now, picture a single weed that seems insignificant at first glance. When left unchecked, this weed grows and spreads, entangling itself around the roots of beautiful plants, sapping their nutrients, and eventually, spreading in the garden even more. This analogy illustrates the dynamics of toxic behavior, which is often subtle and can go unnoticed at first but can infiltrate any type of relationship. Recognizing this to prevent the damage from spreading is vital for nurturing healthy connections.

To free yourself from the hold of toxic relationships, you usually need to have a moment of clarity—a realization that the emotional environment you are in is more harmful than nurturing. This awakening is profound, marking the point where confusion begins to lift, allowing you to see the situation for what it truly is. Realization is powerful and begins the foundation of rebuilding a better relationship. Admitting to yourself that a relationship is toxic does not concede defeat; it is a sign of strength and acknowledging that you deserve better. You see the situation with open eyes and accept that what is happening is not healthy.

If your partner refuses to acknowledge that there is a problem, it is time to begin working on changing this cycle of toxicity. It is a process that, although challenging, is deeply rewarding. When you decide to improve or step away from a relationship that has been draining you, putting yourself first becomes not just a practice but a lifeline. You are reclaiming parts of yourself that may have been neglected or lost. In this crucial time, your top priority is boundary-setting and pursuing joy and peace.

BUILDING BOUNDARIES

Start small. Pick one relationship where you feel a boundary is needed but currently lacking. Determine what this boundary is and plan a conversation to communicate it clearly. If the person refuses by manipulating the circumstances, realize they are unwilling to change and distance yourself from them. Remember, setting boundaries is about self-preservation. When you identify the signs of unhealthy dynamics and understand their unique challenges, you control the relationships that will support your growth and self-respect and contribute to your overall well-being.

Learning to say no is a powerful affirmation of your boundaries.

It conveys respect for yourself and your needs. It can be incredibly challenging, especially if you are used to putting others' needs before your own. Start small by practicing saying no in low-stakes situations to build your confidence. Keep it simple with a straightforward "no" or "I'm not comfortable with that." This is often better and more effective than giving a long explanation.

Use "I" statements to express your needs and feelings without blame. For example, "I need some time to myself" instead of "You're smothering me." Or "I feel hurt when my experiences are dismissed, and I need our conversations to respect my perspective." Frame your boundaries in terms of your own needs and feelings. Don't apologize for your needs. You are unique, and you deserve attention and respect. They might not be able to give it to you, but realize that this is not your fault.

When doubts about your progress or decisions to distance yourself from toxic situations arise, gently remind yourself of the discomfort and pain caused by these circumstances. This reminder is not to dwell on the past but to reinforce the validity of your feelings and the importance of your healing journey.

Remember, you have every right to set boundaries and expect them to be respected.

Setting and maintaining boundaries is essential in all relationships, serving as a guardrail that protects your emotional and mental well-being. Boundaries should be based on mutual respect and understanding. You define what you will and will not accept from others, safeguarding your emotional and mental health. Ask yourself: what specific boundaries must I establish to feel respected and heard in these relationships? How can I communicate these boundaries effectively, and what support do I need to accomplish this? Here are some guidelines.

- **Communicate clearly**: Clarity is key when setting boundaries. Express your needs and limits assertively, ensuring there is no room for misinterpretation. It may mean telling a family member that you need some space to work on personal projects on weekends or informing a friend that their criticism of your choices hurts.
- **Enforcement**: A boundary is only as effective as its enforcement. Be prepared to reinforce your boundaries, showing others that you respect yourself enough to stick to them. Remember, setting boundaries is a sign of self-respect. It teaches others how to treat you and this reflects your worth back at you.
- **Consistency is key**: Uphold your boundaries consistently. People might test or inadvertently cross these limits, especially if they are not accustomed to them. Politely but firmly reiterating your boundaries will reinforce their importance.
- **Practice self-reflection**: Regularly assess your relationships. Ask yourself, "Does this relationship make me feel valued and respected?" If the answer is no, consider ways to address the imbalance or

whether stepping back from the relationship might be healthier.
- **Seek support**: Conversations about boundaries can be challenging. Lean on supportive friends, family, or professionals who can offer advice, encouragement, and perspective. Many articles focus on understanding and implementing healthy boundaries for various types of relationships, which can be found online.
- **Boundary journal**: Keep a journal of the number of times where a boundary was crossed and why. This will help you see how often this occurs and work on changing your strategy to make successful boundaries.

Setting boundaries with an authority figure is challenging but necessary. Sometimes, we have trouble telling our parents, employer, or person in charge "no." This reaction is the unresolved hurt inner child revealing themselves. Now is the time for you to help this inner hurting self. Stand up to the person asserting control and define to them what you will and will not accept from them. Doing this may mean limiting contact with them or having structured interactions where specific topics are off-limits.

It is crucial to communicate these boundaries clearly and assertively with no room for negotiation. Remember, you are not asking for their approval; you're informing them of your terms. If this feels difficult, consider role-playing with a friend or therapist to help build confidence in asserting your boundaries. Practicing what you will say ahead of time can help. Look at yourself in the mirror, saying the script out loud. Notice your posture and look yourself in the eye. The more you do this, the easier it becomes.

Understanding Boundaries for All Relationships

Boundaries are the personal limits we establish to protect ourselves. They act as the invisible fences that protect our emotional and mental garden. They are not barriers to keeping people out but ways to allow us to interact with others while maintaining our safety and respect. Recognizing the significance of boundaries is the first step toward a future where relationships enrich us and not deplete us. Boundaries help us communicate what we are comfortable with and how we wish to be treated by others. Whether it's how much personal information we share or how we allow others to speak to us, boundaries are rooted in our values and our understanding of our worth.

Effectively communicating your boundaries is vital to ensuring they are respected. Choose a calm, neutral time to discuss your boundaries, not in the heat of an argument. Be clear, direct, and assertive without being aggressive. When creating boundaries, you maintain your personal space and privacy. This includes how much physical space you need. Your time is valuable. Boundaries help regulate how much and with whom you spend your time. They also help you decide how much of your emotional and mental energy to invest in various relationships.

Defining a non-negotiable boundary requires identifying the aspects of your life where compromise is not an option. These are your core values, which define yourself and your needs. Identifying your non-negotiables requires introspection and honesty about what truly matters to you. Be as specific as possible about what you need.

MAINTAINING BOUNDARIES

Once your boundaries are set, the real work begins in maintaining them. People may test or unintentionally cross your boundaries, and it's up to you to reinforce them.

- **Check-ins**: Regularly review your boundaries. Are they still serving you? Do they need adjustment?
- **Self-advocacy**: Be prepared to stand up for yourself. If someone crosses a boundary, address it promptly and firmly.
- **Support system**: Lean on friends or a support group for encouragement. Maintaining your boundaries is easier when you have others cheering you on.

Recognize that there will be good days and challenging ones. Be gentle with yourself, allowing space for all your feelings without judgment. In moments of doubt, it's crucial to connect yourself to your values and the goals you are reaching for. Writing things down helps you to see and validate what you are feeling. It will also give you conviction of what is necessary to take your next step.

Remember, setting boundaries is not a one-time task. It is an ongoing negotiation and communication process with yourself and the people in your life. Boundaries honor your needs and support your limits. Staying true to them is the most profound respect you can show yourself. If boundaries are often crossed and maintaining them becomes exhausting, it is time to recognize that separating yourself from this unhealthy relationship is the next step required.

Navigating success on your terms lets you discover that true achievement lies in aligning your actions with your deepest values. When you do, you experience a genuine sense of fulfillment and self-worth. Let go of the need to compare. This can quickly cloud your personal definition of success. The achievements of others do not diminish your own. They are simply different from the path you are walking. By focusing on your journey and growth, you liberate yourself from the cycle of comparison, allowing your unique version of success to flourish.

SEEKING SUPPORT

Once you have acknowledged the reality of your situation, reaching out for support is critical. This network can take many forms, from close friends and family members who have always had your back to professionals who can offer guidance tailored to your needs. Support groups, both in-person and online, can also provide a sense of community and understanding. This network acts as a safety net, offering emotional backing and practical advice as you navigate the complexities of leaving a toxic situation.

- **Friends and family**: These are the ones who know you and care about your well-being. They can offer a listening ear, a place to stay, or even the reassurance that you're making the right decision. Consider

reconnecting with friends or family that you haven't seen for a while.
- **Professionals**: Therapists or counselors specialized in dealing with toxic relationships can provide insights and coping strategies that friends and family might not be able to offer.
- **Support groups**: Connecting with others who have gone through similar experiences can be incredibly validating and empowering. Support networks, whether created in person or online, offer a context of empathy, encouragement, motivation, and common experience. Seek out communities where your story is met with understanding, compassion, and ideas to help you.

Your past may have shaped you, but it does not have to define you.

Your future is created by what you begin today. Though profoundly influencing, past challenges also equip you with power, endurance, and an unmatched potential for empathy and development. Bring acceptance and love to where you are right now. Don't criticize or blame yourself or those who hurt you. Distance yourself from them.

As you create new boundaries, you begin to craft a life rich in respect and fulfillment. Enter the next stage of your journey, prepared to discover and experience a life that fills you with optimism. Each day is a new opportunity to make a life that reflects where you are going and to engage in relationships that bring you joy and fulfillment. The next chapter discusses ways to safely leave toxic relationships and ensure you write life on your terms.

If light is in your heart, you will find your way home.

— RUMI

SEPARATING FROM A TOXIC RELATIONSHIP

The moment you accept what troubles you've been given, the door will open.

— RUMI

Imagine standing on a familiar road that you have walked on for years, knowing each sign and building. Today, you see another path that promises more light, fresh air, and open areas, leading to a better place. This chapter is about seeing that path, understanding any obstacles, and preparing yourself for the journey.

Leaving a toxic environment in the workplace has a few variables to consider. If a coworker creates an unpleasant atmosphere, have an honest conversation with your manager. You may be able to be transferred to a different department or have your schedule changed. If this isn't possible, search for a new job. If your employer is toxic in the work environment, look for a new job that will continue to support you financially. Be prepared to ask a trusted colleague for a positive reference for a future employer because your supervisor may not give you one.

Ending a toxic friendship requires honesty about why your relationship can't continue. The person may not understand your needs, comprehend what is essential to you, or refuse to accept that this relationship drains you. It's important to be clear and concise about your needs to prevent this individual from retaliating or spreading untruths that you 'ghosted' them. If they refuse to accept this, you may have to block their phone number and restrict their access to your social media accounts. Your needs come first. Do not sacrifice them to please others.

A toxic partnership is more complex because of the additional factors involved. Deciding to leave an unhealthy relationship is a pivotal moment. It is when you shift from enduring to acting, from surviving to choosing. This decision takes courage and a deep desire for a healthier, happier life. In a relationship where you cohabitate with this toxic individual, the next steps you take require thought, preparation, and support. These steps will help you create an exit strategy prioritizing your safety, dignity, and future well-being.

PLANNING TO EXIT A TOXIC PARTNERSHIP

Planning your exit from a toxic partnership requires understanding what to do and what to expect. You have been worn down by the toxicity that was invading your life. As you prepare for a new journey in unfamiliar waters, it is essential to feel safe and secure. Thinking ahead will help you navigate this transition.

Consider where you will go, how you will support yourself, and who you can rely on for emotional and practical support. Create a detailed checklist that you can print or save on your phone. It should cover everything from gathering documents to securing accommodations, ensuring you have a clear plan. It also means preparing for potential reactions from your partner and having the strategies necessary to deal with them. When children are involved in this relationship, this requires special attention, which will be covered later in this chapter.

Begin with the end in mind by identifying your ultimate goal. Do you want to move to a new city? Live alone? With friends? Knowing what you are aiming for will help shape your plan. Create a timeline that is realistic in terms of your situation and departure. Set goals for each step in this timeline. This gives structure to your plan and helps you manage the overwhelming task of leaving.

Gathering Essential Documents and Finances

Securing important documents and understanding finances are the essentials as you start over. Gather documents such as your ID, passport, birth certificate, legal papers, and financial records. Keep copies of all important documents in a safe place or with a trusted friend or family member outside your home.

Have a clear list of all financial assets and accounts, including those shared with your partner. This information will be crucial for financial planning and legal considerations. If you have a shared bank account with your partner and haven't done so, open a personal bank account for yourself. This step is vital for establishing financial autonomy. An individual bank account lets you manage your finances confidently and without interference.

Safety, Digital Security, Your Privacy, and Identity Protection

Find a safe place and people who can support you during and after your exit. It can be a friend or family member's home, a shelter, or any place where you feel safe. Reach out to these contacts ahead of time to discuss your plan and ensure they are prepared to help you when the time comes. Have more than one option to guarantee you have somewhere to turn if your first choice falls through. Be transparent. Let your support network know your plans, including when you intend to leave and how they can assist you. When staying with a friend or family member, offer some payment, or if that is not possible, find a way to contribute by doing house or yard work in exchange for the help they are giving you. This begins the process of reclaiming your independence.

In today's digital world, securing your online information is as crucial as locking your front door. Change passwords to all your important accounts, especially if your partner knows them. Consider creating new email accounts and using apps to secure your devices against tracking or surveillance. Abusers often use technology to track or harass their victims, making it essential to take steps to safeguard your information.

- **Secure your devices**: Install or update antivirus and anti-spy software. Change lock codes or patterns on your phone and other personal devices. Consider getting a new phone or changing your phone number. Use secure messaging apps that offer encryption.
- **Change passwords and update privacy settings**: Update passwords for all personal accounts, including email, social media, and financial institutions. Choose passwords that are unrelated to any personal information your partner might know. Review and update the privacy settings on your social media accounts to restrict who can see your posts and personal information.
- **Protect important documents**: Store sensitive documents such as your social security card, passport, and legal papers in a secure location.

ASSESSING FINANCIAL RESOURCES

Financial independence lets you reclaim your life and regain your freedom. Financial resources enable you to stand tall, make choices for your well-being, and move forward confidently. Begin understanding your expenses by tracking your spending to see where your money goes. Include all your bills, groceries, and any discretionary spending. List all your financial assets, savings, investments, and cash reserves. This information is crucial to having a complete picture. Here are practical steps to ensure the stability of a financial plan that supports and maintains your independence:

- **Budgeting**: Track your expenses and create a budget that covers your essentials like rent, food, and utilities, and set some aside for savings. There are budgeting apps or spreadsheets that can help you manage this.
- **Reducing expenses**: Look for areas where you can reduce your spending without impacting your quality of life. A simple change, often overlooked, can free up additional funds for your savings. Switching brands can save money. Become a savvy shopper by checking prices. Each dollar saved builds the foundation for your new life.
- **Savings strategy**: Aim to save a portion of your income regularly, no matter how small. Keep an eye out for the incentives banks offer to open new accounts. Consider setting up an automatic transfer to your savings account each payday. Always look for opportunities that are available.

For many, gaining financial independence means exploring new employment opportunities or enhancing skills to increase your earning potential. Consider:

- **Finding additional work**: A part-time job or freelance work can supplement your income, boost your savings, and accelerate your progress toward independence.
- **Skill development**: Investing in your skills can lead to better-paying jobs. Online courses, workshops, and community college classes are good places to start.

- **Networking**: Reach out to contacts in your desired field. Networking can uncover opportunities that are not advertised publicly.
- **Online platforms**: LinkedIn, job boards, and other community forums can be valuable resources in your search for skill development and employment opportunities.

Looking for Financial Assistance

Sometimes, the path to independence requires external support. Fortunately, there are resources available to those leaving toxic situations:

- **Grants and scholarships**: Look for organizations that offer financial assistance to individuals in your situation. There are scholarships available to help those in difficult circumstances. Large companies often provide opportunities and pay for courses that will further the education of their motivated employees, which can lead to better employment opportunities.
- **Government assistance**: Research government programs designed to help individuals in transition. Check with your local and state agencies. Some of these include housing assistance, food programs, and job training.
- **Non-profit organizations**: Many non-profits offer financial aid, counseling, and other services to help you rebuild. Do not hesitate to ask for help. You are making yourself your number one priority, maybe for the first time in a very long time.

Seeking assistance takes strength and courage. It is a step towards building the life you deserve, free from toxicity and filled with hope. Remember, small steps lead to significant changes in pursuing financial independence. This is not an overnight transformation but gradual progress, each action reinforcing your path to freedom. With each financial decision, you make a stronger safety net, allowing you to move forward more confidently and securely.

UNDERSTANDING LEGAL RIGHTS, RESTRAINING ORDERS AND LEGAL DOCUMENTATION

Familiarizing yourself with your legal rights is crucial. Each person's situation is unique and influenced by local laws and personal circumstances. Begin by researching laws in your area related to domestic relationships, separation, and protection orders. Many regions offer legal protections for individuals seeking to leave abusive or toxic relationships, but the specifics of your location can vary widely.

- **Find reliable sources**: Local government websites, legal aid organizations, and reputable non-profit groups focused on domestic abuse prevention are excellent starting points.
- **Consult legal counsel**: Even a brief consultation with a lawyer can clarify your rights and the legal avenues available to you. There are centers that provide free and low-cost legal services.

In cases where there is a threat to your safety, a restraining order can offer protection. It legally gives you a level of defense to prevent the toxic individual from coming near you or contacting you. Obtaining a restraining order can empower victims to take control of their situation by seeking help from law enforcement and the legal system. It sends a message to the perpetrator that their behavior is unacceptable and will not be tolerated. However, it has limited effectiveness. Some perpetrators may disregard the order and continue to contact the victim. Violating a restraining order is a criminal offense where the perpetrator can face legal consequences, including fines, imprisonment, or additional charges.

- **Burden of proof**: In order to obtain a restraining order, victims often need to provide evidence of harassment, abuse, or threats, which can be challenging, especially in cases where there is no physical evidence or witnesses. Keep a log of any time you felt threatened or other harmful gestures, including the dates, times, and the nature of the incident. This documentation is vital in legal proceedings. Save all text messages and record interactions and conversations with your phone as proof of mistreatment.
- **Understand the process**: The process for obtaining a restraining order can differ by location. Typically, it involves filing paperwork with a court and may require a hearing where both parties are present.
- **Seek support**: The process of obtaining and enforcing a restraining order can be emotionally taxing for victims, as it often involves reliving traumatic experiences and navigating the complexities of the legal system. Local domestic violence organizations often assist in obtaining a

restraining order, handling the paperwork involved, and preparing for court appearances.

WHEN CHILDREN ARE INVOLVED

When leaving an unhealthy relationship with children involved, navigating custody is a complex and emotionally charged situation. There is the decision of custody and visitations. If sole custody is awarded, there is a need for child support. Handling co-parenting arrangements with a toxic ex requires legal and professional advice to ensure that the children's best interests are protected and that your rights are upheld. Understanding your legal rights and obligations in a co-parenting arrangement is crucial for prioritizing the well-being of your children and ensuring their safety and stability.

- **Consult a family lawyer**: A lawyer specializing in family law can advise you on custody matters and help you understand your options and rights. They can provide guidance on your jurisdiction's laws regarding custody and support.
- **Co-parenting counseling**: If your partner is willing to engage in co-parenting counseling, either together or alone, it can provide strategies for handling difficult situations and advice on communicating effectively for the children's sake.
- **Prepare documentation**: Documenting any unhealthy behavior is crucial to establishing the well-being of any children involved. Note instances that demonstrate the other parent's conduct and its

harmful impact on the children to ensure safety measures are put in place.
- **Consider mediation**: In some cases, mediation can be a less adversarial way to reach a custody agreement that serves the children's best interests.

Creating a Co-Parenting Plan with a Toxic Ex

Co-parenting with a toxic ex presents a unique set of challenges that require patience, strategy, and a focus on the children's well-being above all. Successful and effective co-parenting forms when both parties view each other as equally valuable. During personal recovery from a toxic relationship, transitioning into a co-parenting arrangement demands respect, support, precise planning, robust boundaries, and an unwavering commitment to maintaining a stable environment for the children involved.

Children need to be reassured that they are loved and safe. Open dialogs are crucial for their well-being. Be honest with yourself and be honest with them. Let them know you are actively working on improving difficult situations and follow through by seeking the help and support you need to navigate the separation. During this time, self-care is vital for maintaining your ability to cope.

Focus on the endgame. A well-thought-out co-parenting plan is the foundation for successful co-parenting. It is the clear blueprint that outlines how you and your ex-partner will share responsibilities and make decisions for your children. This plan must consider the children's daily routines, education, healthcare, and emotional needs, ensuring they have a consistent and secure upbringing.

- **Using a mediator**: Sometimes, direct communication with a toxic ex can be counterproductive. Involving a neutral third party who specializes in family law can help facilitate the creation of a balanced co-parenting plan.
- **Attention on logistics**: Concentrate on practical arrangements like schedules, pick-up times, and methods of communication regarding the children's needs. This approach helps keep discussions objective and focused on the children's well-being.
- **Flexibility within structure**: While the plan should provide a clear structure, some flexibility is also necessary to accommodate the inevitable changes in schedules and circumstances.

Boundaries for Co-parenting

Setting and maintaining firm boundaries with a toxic ex is critical in co-parenting. These boundaries help protect your emotional well-being and ensure that your interactions remain focused on the children's needs rather than personal conflicts.

- **Define communication channels**: Agree on specific channels for all co-parenting communications, such as email or a co-parenting app. This can help avoid unnecessary personal contact and keep conversations documented.
- **Limit personal information**: Share only what is necessary regarding the children's welfare. Avoid discussing personal matters or details beyond the scope of co-parenting.

- **Scheduled updates**: Establish regular intervals for updates on the children, such as weekly emails or messages through a co-parenting app. This keeps both parents informed without the need for constant back-and-forth communication.
- **When your ex bad mouths you**: In a case like this, talk to your children first, saying that when upset emotions are involved, hurtful things can be said. Speak to your ex and point out that pitting parents against each other harms the children. If this doesn't change anything, contact your lawyer. Parental alienation is a form of abuse. Have conversations with your children, saying that you are working to resolve any conflicts that arise in the best way possible.
- **Keep it civil**: Do not slander your ex. You may feel like you are standing up for yourself but do not say or post derogatory comments on social media. Reserve negative comments for confidential conversations between you and your therapist or a trusted friend. Your words can be used against you in court.

Getting Support for Your Children

Children are often the most affected by the breakup of their parent's relationship, and they need ample support to navigate the changes in their family dynamics.

- **Open conversations**: Encourage children to express their feelings about the changes in their family setup. Listen actively and validate their emotions,

reassuring them that both parents love them and will continue to be there for them. If your ex is unavailable for the children, tell them it is not their fault and that the ex-partner is working on improving.
- **Consistency across households**: As much as possible, aim for consistency in rules, discipline, and routines across both households. A toxic partner may continue to try to manipulate things. Keep records of conversations and transactions, including the dates and details. Your ex may spoil the children. If this upsets you, stay calm and maintain your composure. Your reaction may be confusing to the children. Your aim is to help them feel secure and not experience any extra confusion. Calming techniques will be discussed in chapter seven.
- **Professional support for children**: Children will benefit from speaking to a counselor or therapist who can help them process their feelings in a safe and supportive environment. They may need reassurance that the breakup was not their fault and that they do not have to take or choose sides. A child may experience loyalty conflicts and not want to see one of their parents. They could feel guilt, shame, or blame that needs to be addressed.

Co-parenting with a toxic ex is a delicate balance between protecting your well-being and ensuring the best for your children. Seeking legal and professional advice helps set firm boundaries in place. You create a stable and positive environment that supports your children by focusing on a well detailed co-parenting plan.

WHEN ANIMALS ARE IN THE EQUATION

Our animals are our support system. For some of us, they are our 'children'. Their unconditional love has helped us get through difficult times. When there is an animal involved in a toxic relationship, consider their care. Ask yourself, who gets custody of this loyal and dependent creature? Determine who legally owns the animal and who has been primarily responsible for its care. Do you think your ex-partner will neglect it? Prioritize the welfare and best interests of the animal above your personal interests and needs. Think about the animal's emotional attachment to both parties and strive to maintain continuity and stability. If the animal is jointly owned, decide whether joint custody or a shared visitation schedule is feasible.

Consider formalizing any agreements regarding ownership, custody, visitation, and financial responsibilities through legal documentation by drafting a pet custody agreement or co-ownership agreement and have it notarized. If disagreements arise or emotions run high, seek the assistance of a mediator or counselor experienced in pet custody to facilitate constructive communication and negotiation.

Care for Your Animals During the Separation

Develop a plan to help the animal adjust to changes in its environment, living arrangements, and routines. Gradually introduce your animal companion to its new environment to minimize stress and anxiety. Have something familiar for it, like a familiar food dish or bed. Talk to your animal like you do to a child. They are wiser than you may think. Let them know that a transition is happening and there will be some changes, but they will always be cared for.

Ask friends, family, or coworkers if they can temporarily help during this time. If they cannot, there are agencies available for instances like this. Red Rover is a non-profit animal rescue organization that helps victims of abuse find temporary shelter for pets and can even assist financially with their care. Search the options available to you.

There will be challenges, but knowing your rights is empowering. Using all the resources available will assist you in navigating this transition. Recognize this is a pivotal point in your life. With a clear understanding, you make each step of this journey one where you and any children involved can grow and thrive. These actions form the foundation for a safer, healthier future.

> *We do not have to became heroes overnight. Just a step at a time, meeting each thing that comes up, seeing it not as dreadful as it appeared, discovering we have the strength to stare it down.*
>
> — ELEANOR ROOSEVELT

DEALING WITH THE AFTERMATH

You never know how strong you are until being strong is your only choice.

— BOB MARLEY

Leaving a toxic relationship often does not mark the end of challenges. Instead, it might begin a different kind of struggle, an angry backlash, and manipulation from the ex-partner as they try to hold on to you and claw their way back into your life. Preparing for this possibility will help you handle the backlash and manipulation post-breakup. Awareness equips you with resilience and the tactics you need to maintain your newfound freedom and peace.

When you decide to walk away from a toxic relationship, you might unknowingly create a defensive reaction in your ex-partner, which causes them to strategically employ antics to pull you back into the chaos. It's not uncommon for a surge of attempts to contact you, make promises of change, or spread falsehoods about you in your social circles.

This is how they try to regain control rather than a genuine desire to mend ways. Recognizing that this behavior is more manipulation rather than a genuine attempt at reconciliation is crucial. An increase in messages, unexpected visits, or public displays of affection following your decision are warning flags. Mentally prepare yourself for these scenarios by reminding yourself why you left. Revisiting your reasons can solidify your resolve when faced with this situation.

STAYING FIRM IN YOUR DECISION AND FINDING YOUR SUPPORT SYSTEM

The cornerstone of maintaining your distance from a toxic ex lies in the strength of your conviction. Staying firm in your decision, especially when faced with manipulation or guilt-tripping, is a testament to your self-respect and commitment to a healthier life.

- **Solidify your resolve**: Write a letter to yourself detailing the pain and reasons that led to your departure. When in doubt, reading this letter can be a powerful reminder of your journey towards self-respect.
- **Limit interaction**: If possible, limit direct communication. Using email or text messages for necessary communication allows you to have control over when and how you respond, reducing the emotional impact.

In the aftermath of leaving a toxic relationship, understanding that the manipulation can continue is crucial to being mentally and emotionally prepared. By anticipating potential backlash, you can stay firm in your decision and keep yourself protected. Your awareness creates the buffer against these tactics, safeguarding your well-being and ensuring your journey toward a healthier life remains uninterrupted. In some cases, the backlash may escalate to a point where legal intervention becomes necessary. Keeping a detailed record of any interactions with your ex-partner, especially those that are threatening or harassing, is essential. The necessity of documentation is crucial in maintaining the ground you have gained.

- **Maintain records**: Keep screenshots of messages, log phone calls, and save emails. These documents can serve as evidence should you seek a restraining order or legal protection.
- **Legal documentation**: In extreme cases, these records can be invaluable in legal proceedings, providing clear evidence of your ex-partner's behavior.

The turbulence following a breakup from a toxic relationship reinforces the importance of having a supportive circle. Friends and family are your first line of defense, offering emotional and sometimes financial support. It's important to communicate openly, share your feelings and concerns, and let them know what support you need. They can offer a shoulder to cry on or a couch to crash on when things get tough. These trusted individuals can provide their perspective, reassurance, and validation when you are feeling uncertain and can offer the encouragement needed for you to stay the course. They can provide stability, guidance, and the occasional reality check needed to move forward.

Sometimes, friends and family might not always be equipped with the best advice for complex emotional situations. This is where support groups and professional help come in. Support groups give you the opportunity to connect with others who have faced similar challenges, which can be incredibly validating. These groups provide a sense of community and understanding that friends and family might not be able to offer. Therapists or counselors can offer insights and coping strategies and provide a neutral, safe space to process feelings and plan the next steps.

SETTING BOUNDARIES WITH MUTUAL FRIENDS AND FAMILY

Navigating the waters of mutual relationships after leaving a toxic relationship creates another set of challenges and the need to re-evaluate these friendships. It is human nature to take or choose sides. The steps you take to establish boundaries with mutual friends and family are delicate yet crucial. These boundaries honor your needs while maintaining friendships from the shared relationship.

In creating boundaries, finding a balance between honesty about your situation and respect for their relationship with the other person involves both clarity and assertiveness. Here is how you can approach this:

- **Be clear and direct**: When explaining your situation, be clear about what you are comfortable

sharing regarding the breakup and what is off-limits. Let them know your personal feelings are fragile and need to be supported in a delicate manner.
- **Express your needs**: Let them know what assistance you need. This might include asking them not to relay information about your ex to you or not inviting you to the same gatherings.
- **Use "I" statements**: Framing your needs around "I" statements helps keep the conversation focused on your feelings and needs without making accusatory statements about the other person.

In the aftermath of a toxic breakup, your story, experiences, and feelings are fragile and precious. Protecting this narrative is crucial for maintaining privacy and preserving your journey toward healing. When interacting with mutual friends and family:

- **Decide what to share**: Before conversations, decide what aspects of your story you are comfortable sharing. This helps maintain control over your narrative.
- **Request discretion**: If you choose to share details with someone, ask for their discretion upfront. Make it clear that you're sharing confidently and that this is not information you want to be circulated.
- **Be prepared for questions**: Mutual friends and family might have questions. Prepare a few responses in advance for inquiries you are not comfortable answering. A simple "I'm not ready to talk about that right now" is perfectly acceptable.

Loyalty conflicts are almost inevitable when mutual friends and family are involved.

Some mutual friends may feel torn between you and your ex-partner, while others might unconsciously choose sides. To support your growth and well-being, clearly state what you expect and what is off-limits for discussions. When any loyalty conflicts arise, do your best to manage them with empathy but not allow yourself to be on the receiving end of any animosity. Sometimes, it is best to let go of certain relationships. Your ex might try to drag your name through the mud, painting you as the villain. Remember, as you move through this process, protect your personal narrative and reassess which relationships align with your renewed sense of self. Handling these mutual friendships with grace involves:

- **Accepting their position**: Understand that some friends and family might struggle with their loyalties. It is important to recognize their feelings without pressuring them to take sides.
- **Seeking neutral ground**: For those who wish to remain friends with both parties, suggest neutral settings for interactions that do not involve discussions about the breakup or your ex-partner.
- **Focusing on supportive relationships**: Invest more deeply in relationships with friends and family who provide the understanding and support you need during this time.

Leaving a toxic relationship often brings clarity not just about that relationship but about others in your life as well.

This clarity might reveal that some mutual relationships no longer align with the person you are becoming. To re-evaluate these relationships:

- **Reflect on their impact**: Consider whether each relationship supports your well-being and growth. Do these friends and family members respect your boundaries? Do they offer the support and understanding you need?
- **Give yourself permission to step back**: It's okay to distance yourself from relationships that drain your energy or pull you back towards negative patterns. This does not have to be a dramatic cutting of ties but the act of investing less time from the emotionally draining person.
- **Focus on reciprocity**: Seek out and nurture reciprocal relationships where support and understanding flow both ways. These connections will sustain and uplift you as you move forward.

ONLINE AND COMMUNITY RESOURCES AND SEEKING PROFESSIONAL HELP

Asking for help may be difficult when you have become a victim of manipulation. The strength found in a community, a kind word from a friend, or understanding from a professional can brighten the way. Rebuilding your self-esteem comes from the support, encouragement, and validation of others. Therapists, support groups, and trusted friends can offer perspectives that reaffirm your worth and assist in navigating the complex emotions tied to healing.

The internet has revolutionized the way we seek and find support. Teladoc gives you access to a doctor almost instantly. Online forums are a place to ask questions and get answers, ideas, and opinions. There are social media groups and websites dedicated to healing from toxic relationships that can offer resources, advice, support, and camaraderie from the safety of your keyboard. Local community centers, libraries, and non-profits often host events, workshops, and support groups for those dealing with relationship issues. They can also provide support and education on building a life after a toxic relationship.

Protecting your privacy and safety while seeking support is of utmost importance. When engaging with support groups or professionals, ensure that confidentiality agreements are in place. Be cautious about sharing identifiable information in online forums or social media groups, especially if there's a risk your toxic partner might be monitoring your activities.

- **Choosing safe platforms**: Search for support groups and forums that prioritize their members' privacy and have clear guidelines to protect users.
- **Private browsing**: If you are concerned about your partner monitoring your internet usage, use private browsing features or secure messaging apps when seeking support online.

Therapy Options for Support

If you find yourself overwhelmed by emotions, struggling to make decisions, or if the thought of leaving fills you with unbearable anxiety, seek professional help. Finding a therapist who specializes in toxic relationships or trauma can be particularly beneficial, as they understand the dynamics of such experiences. These professionals act as guides through the emotional landscape of leaving a toxic relationship, offering tools and strategies to cope with the change.

They can help untangle the complex feelings of guilt, fear, and relief that often accompany such a significant life shift. Finding the right therapist can take some research. Look for someone experienced in dealing with the issues like yours. Websites like Psychology Today offer directories that filter therapists by specialty, location, and insurance.

Finding the right therapist is like meeting someone who speaks your language and understands you. They can provide ways to reach the roots of any diminished self-esteem and rebuild your sense of self-worth. Friends who understand and respect your journey can offer the encouragement needed to bolster your self-esteem.

There are many options available in therapy, each one a gem offering a different path to healing. It is important to realize that therapy is not a one-size-fits-all remedy but a personalized journey toward your wellness. This involves the best approach that works for you and resonates with your inner self. It should feel like it is just what you need on your path to healing. Somatic therapy has you focus on physical sensations and use mind-body exercises to help release painful emotions. Research what is best for you. Your doctor can also suggest which would be the most helpful for your needs. Here are a few types of therapy to consider:

- **Cognitive behavioral therapy (CBT)** focuses on reshaping unhealthy thought patterns to help change reactive behaviors and responses. It offers coping skills to tackle problems and create positive thoughts to replace negative thinking. The 3 Cs introduced to help focus on developing new thoughts are: Catch it, Check it, and Change it.
- **Dialectical behavior therapy (DBT)** This method combines the mindfulness of CBT principles with talking. This helps to regulate emotions more easily. It introduces mindfulness and stress tolerance for people who feel their emotions intensely and helps manage these strong emotions.
- **Trauma-informed therapy**: Trauma affects a person's ability to cope. This therapy is tailored for individuals who are healing from trauma by giving them a safe environment to work in and to learn coping skills. Safety, learning to trust, being empowered, and choice are emphasized in this therapy to help heal individuals who have been traumatized.

Addressing the many different layers of damage caused by unhealthy relationships can be vastly helped by using several different forms of therapy. Working with several therapies can offer a more significant, in-depth approach to healing. You can utilize CBT for the day-to-day thought repatterning while engaging in trauma-informed therapy for the deeper emotional wounds. Find the right tools that work for you, embracing them as your allies on your journey to rediscovering your essence.

In its many forms, therapy offers a sanctuary and is a place where healing begins. It helps with understanding and evolves into transformation. These tools will grow and change as you become more confident in yourself. Therapy will give you insights not just into your past but into the limitless potential of your future, a future where you stand taller, healed, and whole. As you transition from navigating the immediate aftermath of a breakup into the broader horizons of rebuilding and growth, you are reaffirming your commitment to yourself and the future that you are building.

I can be changed by what happens to me. But I refuse to be reduced by it.

— MAYA ANGELOU

Part Three
REGAINING YOUR WORTH

REWRITING YOUR STORY-BEGIN HEALING THE EMOTIONAL WOUNDS

*Don't look for the remedy for your troubles outside yourself.
You are the medicine; you are the cure for your own sorrow.*

— RUMI

Visualize that you are in a movie theater with the lights dimmed, and your life story starts to appear on the screen. What are you seeing? Is it a drama filled with challenges, a plot full of twists and turns, or a tale of triumph? Imagine you can edit this movie, reshape scenes, and even alter the storyline. This chapter is not just about viewing your life as a narrative; it is about seizing the director's chair and actively rewriting your story to reflect the person you aspire to be.

UNDERSTANDING AND CHANGING NEGATIVE NARRATIVES

Our lives are a collection of stories we tell ourselves. These stories are the product of our experiences. They shape our identity, decisions, and how we view the world. These scripts we follow often unconsciously govern our actions and reactions. For instance, if your narrative is that you are always the one who gets overlooked, this belief will create the dynamic of how you interact in relationships, at work, and in social settings. It may hold you back from voicing your opinion or pursuing opportunities because the storyline you have internalized tells you it won't make a difference.

Think of a comment that a family member or friend said that stuck with you. Perhaps it was a remark like, "You're not the outgoing type." Over time, this single sentence evolved into a defining part of your character, influencing how you interact socially. You have the power to challenge and change these narratives within you. It starts with identifying these stories and asking, "Is this truly me, or is it a narrative I've inherited?" This process is not to assign blame but to recognize that some chapters of your story might have been written based on others' perceptions and that you are the one who can rewrite them.

Identifying Inherited Narratives:

- **List**: Write down statements or beliefs about yourself that you have always assumed to be true.
- **Source**: Next to each, note where or who they might have come from.
- **Truth check**: For each statement, ask yourself, "Is this genuinely me, or is it someone else's view?"

Consider situations where you felt disrespected or uncomfortable. Think about and define what boundary was crossed. Understanding what you value most will help you identify where you cannot afford to compromise. Write down and keep a list of your non-negotiable boundaries as a reminder and guide when entering new relationships.

Transformational Activity:

Create a two-column chart where you list "Old Narrative" statements and their "New Narrative" counterparts. Write your past experiences and then rewrite how you envision your life to be. This visual comparison helps you see who you are and what you want in life as you rewrite your script, the new life story as you move forward.

REWRITING THE STORY, THE JOURNEY OF RE-PARENTING YOURSELF

Rewriting your story is an act of empowerment. It involves consciously choosing which parts of your narrative serve you and which ones need to be rewritten. This doesn't mean denying your past or the challenges that you have faced. It's letting you see them as steps in your growth. For example, instead of seeing yourself as a victim of circumstance, you choose to view your experiences as lessons that have built resilience and wisdom. This shift does not happen overnight. This process begins with small edits—a decision to try something new, stand up for yourself, or change a long-held belief about what you can achieve.

Re-parenting is a healing process that involves giving yourself the love, care, compassion, and guidance you may not have received or were denied during your childhood. At its core, re-parenting is based on the idea of stepping in as the best parent you needed but did not have. It means being the nurturer, attending to your emotional and physical well-being with kindness and patience, providing comfort and care, and offering encouragement.

Focusing on healing the inner child can unlock doors to understanding and heal deeply rooted emotional pain. Every stage of life can hold multiple aspects of hurt and painful memories. Each hurtful moment needs to be acknowledged and the story rewritten so that you are now the loving and reassuring caretaker to the sad inner child within you. When you notice that you are reacting to a situation, this means there is still a charge to it. This is a chance to pause, be the observer, the witness, and reflect to understand your feelings. As you identify the emotion, think of where it originated from. This awareness gives you the opportunity to acknowledge it, accept it, and bring loving energy to yourself, which will help release the charge.

This approach is crucial for healing because it addresses deep-seated emotional needs, allowing you to develop a healthier relationship with yourself. As you do this method, acknowledge that although you cannot change your past, you can nurture your inner child in the present moment, providing the emotional support needed to heal from past wounds.

Parenting yourself is finding and listening to all the different aspects and versions of the neglected inner child residing within you.

This process is pivotal for anyone who has experienced neglect or emotional abuse or grew up in an environment where their needs were not adequately met. Embarking on the re-parenting journey is a profound act of self-love and healing. It requires patience, dedication, and sometimes the courage to seek support. Through this process, you mend the wounds of the past and lay the foundation for a future where you can thrive, guided by a sense of inner peace and self-compassion.

Steps in the Re-parenting Process

The journey of re-parenting oneself unfolds in several deliberate steps, each designed to heal inner child wounds:

- **Acknowledgment**: The first step is acknowledging the presence of your inner child and their unmet needs. This means delving through all the stages of your childhood. As the memories of each inner child appear to you, talk to them and tell them they are safe and loved now. Give them the attention and affection that was missing. Recognize the moments of neglect and lack of support as your consciousness becomes aware of them. Acknowledge the pain. Tell your hurting selves that was the past and you are here for them now.
- **Communication**: Begin a dialogue with your inner child. You might write letters to them or talk to them in your mind, offering words of comfort, understanding, and acceptance. Tell them that you know they hurt, but you are now here for them. Pay close attention and notice if they are ready to hear you or if they need more time. Trust may need to be rebuilt.
- **Meeting needs**: Identify what your inner child needs now. It could be safety, validation, fun, or love, and find ways to fulfill these needs. This could mean

setting aside time for play, allowing yourself to explore new hobbies, practicing self-affirmations and words of encouragement.
- **Setting boundaries**: Part of re-parenting involves showing your inner child that you are setting healthy boundaries by learning to say no, honoring your limits, and protecting your energy. These boundaries will offer your inner child the safety and security that were missing in the past and begin to build trust in yourself.

Internal Anger and Its Effects

Anger is a natural response to being treated unfairly and not being heard or validated. However, the victim may turn this anger inward, blaming themselves for the situation. This can lead to feelings of guilt and shame, further exacerbating the internal anger. While anger itself is a natural emotion, when it's consistently suppressed or ignored, it can lead to various physical issues, such as high blood pressure, heart disease, and a weakened immune system. It can also lead to mental health issues like depression and anxiety.

Suppressed anger is like a pressure cooker, slowly building up steam until it reaches a breaking point.

The victim may become overly defensive. In some cases, the victim may resort to self-destructive behaviors, such as substance abuse or self-harm, to cope with the intense feelings of anger and frustration. When anger surfaces, it is imperative to acknowledge it and not ignore or suppress it again. It is vital to your healing journey to allow yourself to feel your emotions. Feel the anger, but don't stay angry.

Accept this as part of the healing process. Have conversations with the anger. Acknowledge the cause of it and release it. Realize that holding onto anger only hurts you.

Intense physical activity can work off some of the pent-up rage. Engage in vigorous exercise or activities. Punching a pillow is a good physical release. Find a place where you can yell. Once you get past the energy brought on by rage, begin now to focus more on mindfulness. Practice deep breathing exercises to calm the nervous system and release tension. Write about your feelings of anger in a journal to express and process them. It's essential to recognize that anger is a normal emotion, and learning to manage it effectively, rather than suppressing it, is crucial for your overall well-being.

Self-Soothing Techniques

Integrating self-soothing techniques is a vital aspect of re-parenting, as these methods provide immediate comfort and relief to the inner child:

- **Deep, relaxed breathing**: Simple and very effective, deep, slow breathing calms the nervous system and reduces feelings of anxiety or distress. Awareness of your breath cultivates the connection of your mind and inner self. Mindful breathing allows self-reflection and is the cornerstone of meditation.
- **Emotional freedom technique** (EFT) or Tapping: EFT involves tapping on specific pressure points while focusing on emotions or memories, helping to release emotional pain. There are YouTube videos that can guide you through this, or you can seek

professional help. As you tap on the pressure points, you say what has upset you, acknowledging the feeling and the intensity of it. Each time, you end with an empowering statement of self-acceptance and repeat this until the upsetting emotion has lessened or become neutralized.

- **Creative expression**: The importance of creativity cannot be overstated. Drawing, painting, or writing are therapeutic outlets for emotions your inner child has not been allowed to express verbally. It helps open the mind and get in touch with a part of us that has been lost. Creativity helps us solve problems more effectively and to think outside the box. It allows us to be more adaptable to change.
- **Physical comfort**: Touch is the most fundamental human need we all have. It soothes the limbic system, the part of the brain that involves memory, emotion, and stress. Physical contact improves the immune system. The healing effects of touch are monumental in recovery. The inner child who has been denied the love and warmth they so desperately needed requires a hug. Physically hug yourself or wrap yourself in a warm blanket. Hold yourself tight. Give yourself a bear hug. Taking a soothing bath can provide physical comfort. Pet an animal. If you don't have one, consider volunteering at an animal shelter or horse farm. Go for a massage. Physical touch not only soothes the recipient but also helps the person giving it. Open yourself up to hugging a dear friend or a family member.

Assertiveness Training

As you learn to love yourself, you begin to respect who you are. Being assertive is the voice of self-respect. As you do this, you are giving your inner child the support they need. Communicating your worth to the people in your life ensures that your needs and boundaries are being heard and respected. Developing assertiveness is like strengthening a muscle—the more you practice, the stronger it becomes.

Let yourself express your views and opinions about something you believe in, especially when you might typically stay silent. A toxic relationship has made you think that your needs or opinions don't matter. When speaking up, you form a way to validate your thoughts and feelings. Exercise your right to decline requests or invitations that don't align with your values or well-being. It is OK to say no. Remember, "no" is a complete sentence.

One of the main barriers to assertive communication is the fear of conflict or possible negative consequences, like getting fired from your job for speaking up. There are techniques and classes available that give you guidelines and pointers on how to speak to other people in a diplomatic way. Remember and understand that your body language is a non-verbal form of communication. Your posture and eye contact are ways of expressing your confidence. Stand tall and look the person in the eye as you speak to them.

When it comes to assertiveness, there are the 3 Cs to remember: Confident, Clear, and Controlled. These words are helpful reminders to express yourself assertively. When you are confident, you believe in your ability to handle the situation and maintain your composure. Clearly state what you expect without raising your voice. Make sure your message is easy to understand and is not exaggerated. Sometimes, you can be triggered by a memory, which can stir up strong emotions affecting your behavior. At times like this, take control by pausing and taking a breath to compose yourself. Request what you need, whether support, space, or understanding, and become comfortable with asking for what you need. Doing this is a fundamental aspect of advocating for yourself.

OVERCOMING SELF-DOUBT AND BUILDING A HEALTHY SELF-ESTEEM

Self-doubt is the shadow that dims the light of self-respect. It whispers uncertainties and fears, challenging your belief in your worth. Self-doubt began when a seed was planted by someone telling you that you were wrong when you were right. Overcoming self-doubt requires consciously replacing these negative narratives with affirmations of your capabilities and value.

- **Challenge negative thoughts**: When self-doubt creeps in, challenge it with evidence of your achievements and strengths. Keep a "victory log" to document both your big and small successes.
- **Seek constructive feedback**: Instead of shying away from feedback, seek it out from trusted sources. Use it as a tool to grow, reminding yourself that learning and development are signs of strength, not weakness.
- **Celebrate effort, not just the outcome**: Recognize the effort you put into your endeavors, your strength, and your determination to accomplish your desired goals. By valuing the process as much as the

result, you reinforce your worth and belief in your abilities.

In the aftermath of enduring a toxic relationship, the mirror you look into often reflects a distorted image that has been tainted by experiences and has chipped away at your self-esteem. When you prioritize yourself, you flourish, which leads to a healthier self-image. Bring acceptance and love to where you are right now. This sets the stage for focusing on where you want to go. Rebuilding your self-esteem takes time and effort and begins with:

- **Identifying strengths**: Start by listing your strengths, no matter how small they may seem. Regularly remind yourself of these, especially in moments of doubt.
- **Setting achievable goals**: Accomplishing goals, even minor ones, can significantly boost your self-worth. Begin with small, manageable goals to build a sense of achievement.
- **Positive affirmations**: Incorporate affirmations that resonate with how you desire to view yourself. Regularly repeating phrases like "I have all I need to change my story" will gradually reshape your internal dialogue.
- **Engaging in activities that reflect your worth:** Invest time in activities that make you feel valuable and fulfilled, whether volunteering, creative pursuits, or learning new skills.
- **Surrounding yourself with positivity**: Choose to spend time with people who uplift you and reflect the qualities you admire and aspire to embody.

Self-Compassion

Self-compassion is essential to self-esteem, allowing for growth even in the face of adversity. Practicing self-compassion involves:

- **Acknowledgment of pain**: Recognize and accept your feelings of pain or inadequacy without judgment. Understand that suffering is a part of the human experience, not a reflection of your worth.
- **Kindness toward yourself**: Be as kind to yourself as you would be to a dear friend facing similar challenges. Replace self-criticism with supportive and understanding language.
- **Accepting coping mechanisms without shame**: Understand that coping mechanisms, even those that no longer serve you, were developed for survival. Approach them with curiosity rather than judgment, exploring their origin and gently guiding yourself towards healthier strategies.

Remember that each step taken, each moment of self-care, and every act of self-compassion is a brick laid on the path to a restored and resilient sense of self. This process is not marked by erasing past pains but by the growth that rises from them, giving a testament to your strength and capacity for renewal.

SEEKING PROFESSIONAL HELP

While the journey of re-parenting can be initiated on your own, there are times when professional guidance can significantly enhance the healing process. This guidance offers tips on how to process and integrate your experiences in a way that strengthens your sense of self.

A therapist can understand you and your experiences without judgment, help you process what you have gone through, and encourage you to heal and move forward in your life. They can introduce new perspectives and coping strategies and allow for deep changes that align with your aspirations and values. They can also help you identify the themes and patterns in your narrative that no longer serve you.

Seek help when you feel stuck in a negative self-narrative you can't break free from. If past traumas and experiences weigh heavily on you and you are unsure how to heal them, look for outside help.

If you find yourself struggling to connect with your inner child, or if the emotions that surface feel overwhelming, choose a therapist to offer support, validation, and strategies for navigating the complex emotions that arise during re-parenting. Therapy can provide a structured approach to re-parenting, offering insights into your emotional patterns and behaviors. A therapist can guide you in developing self-soothing techniques, setting boundaries, and progressively healing your inner child.

Finding the Right Therapist

Seek a therapist who has experience in childhood trauma and re-parenting. A good therapist should make you feel seen, heard, and safe to explore your inner child's needs. The bond formed between you and your therapist is the cornerstone of effective therapy. This connection goes beyond mere comfort and is about feeling seen and understood.

Look for a therapist whose personality and approach align with your own. You may have to try out a few therapists before finding the right match. Find a therapist you feel entirely comfortable with, who encourages open dialogue, listens attentively, and genuinely understands your experiences and perspectives.

CELEBRATING SMALL VICTORIES AND ACKNOWLEDGING PROGRESS

Small victories often pave the way for monumental change in healing and self-growth. Whether it is the first morning you wake up feeling a bit lighter, or the moment you realize that a comment that once hurt doesn't sting as much, these are the milestones worth celebrating.

- **Positive reinforcement:** Start or end your day by listing three small achievements or positive moments. This can be as simple as cooking a meal for yourself, setting a boundary, or even getting out of bed when you do not feel like it.
- **Visual reminders**: A great way to see your accomplishments is to write down whenever you achieve a goal, no matter how small, on a piece of paper and put it in a jar. Over time, you will collect a tangible representation of your achievements, which can be incredibly motivating.
- **Celebrate milestones**: Set up rewards for yourself as you reach certain milestones. This could be as simple

as a relaxing bath, a day out in nature, or watching your favorite movie—whatever feels like a treat.

Recognizing and rejoicing in these moments fuels your journey forward and transforms your relationship with yourself. It's like planting seeds of joy and watching as they grow into a garden of self-esteem and motivation. This acknowledgment is more than a pat on the back—it allows you to pause and notice the subtle shifts in your thoughts and actions that signal you are moving in the right direction, reminding you that healing is not only about the destination but also about appreciating the journey.

Self-celebration is crucial in reinforcing self-worth.

It is a way of telling yourself that your efforts matter and are worthy of joy and praise. This practice can significantly boost self-esteem and be a powerful antidote to self-doubt. Develop small rituals of celebration. Light a special candle, play your favorite song, or do a little dance every time you achieve a goal. Make the act of celebration a joyful and regular part of your routine.

Sharing your successes with trusted friends or support groups is an act of acknowledgment. It reinforces your achievements, reminding you that you're not alone in your journey. When you vocalize your victories, you validate your efforts and invite others to join in your celebration, creating a cycle of positive reinforcement and encouragement.

- **Find your cheerleaders**: Identify friends, family members, or support group members who

understand your journey and are genuinely happy to celebrate your successes with you.
- **Sharing is caring**: Remember, when you share your successes, you inspire and motivate others in their journey. It is a way of paying it forward, spreading positivity and hope.

As you celebrate small victories on the road of healing, remember that every step forward, no matter how small, is a testament to your resilience and determination. By acknowledging progress, you choose to navigate your path to recovery and leave a trail of joy and confidence in your wake.

Embrace the lessons of this chapter, letting them be part of your life as you continue to grow, heal, and transform. In the following chapters, we will delve deeper into the practices that support your journey to a life filled with self-compassion, fulfillment, and love.

> *Always remember you are braver than you believe, stronger than you seem, smarter than you think, and twice as beautiful as you'd ever imagined.*
>
> — RUMI

SELF-COMPASSION AND DEEPER HEALING

Give yourself a kiss. If you want to hold the beautiful one, hold yourself to yourself.

— RUMI

Imagine a garden full of flowers. Every blossom represents different aspects of your life—your career, relationships, hobbies, and dreams. Now, think about what happens when you water these plants with self-compassion instead of self-criticism. They thrive, right? This chapter is your watering can.

Navigating the turbulence of toxic relationships is no small feat. Allow yourself to acknowledge the pain, confusion, and doubt that was created by the manipulation. These emotions and feelings cause you to lose trust and question your ability. Every step taken towards nurturing your self-esteem is a vital step in your journey of healing. You are reclaiming your narrative and moving beyond your past experiences.

Recognizing the impact of a toxic relationship and engaging in self-love will help you develop a new sense of worth and value. Acknowledging your resilience and capacity to endure and adapt shows an indomitable spirit that deserves recognition and celebration. Your story becomes a testament to an inner strength that you may not have considered, and this awareness enables you to move forward from your past experiences of surviving to a future of thriving.

SELF-CARE AND SELF-COMPASSION

In this time of realization, self-care is not just beneficial; it's necessary. You put yourself first, your oxygen mask on first, ensuring you are emotionally and physically equipped to handle the challenges ahead. Self-care is the anchor that keeps you grounded amidst the storms of life. It is a reminder that you truly matter. There are many self-care techniques to work with. The key is to intentionally carve out time every day to attend to your well-being. This self-care is more than just physical; it includes acknowledging fears that arise and understanding that they are a natural response to past abuse. By prioritizing self-care, you are acknowledging your worth and valuing yourself.

Self-compassion is the practice of treating yourself with the same kindness and understanding you would give to a good friend in need. It includes hugging yourself when you stumble instead of any negative self-talk. Toxic relationships often leave us with a harsh inner critic, the stern voice inside us that constantly criticizes and belittles us. Choose encouraging words over criticism and growth over guilt. Accepting that you are not perfect and practicing self-compassion nurtures your growth after a toxic relationship. It is a gentle reminder that you are doing your best, and sometimes, that is everything.

The practice of self-compassion also involves letting go of comparison thinking. When you do this, you convey a message of self-respect to your psyche. Turn kindness inward. When faced with comparison thinking, remind yourself of your progress and successes, and practice gratitude for everything you are learning and achieving. By embracing self-compassion, you are honoring yourself and allowing healing and growth. As you water your garden with self-compassion, watch as every part of your life begins to bloom more, reflecting the love and care you are giving to yourself.

Breaking the Self-Criticism Cycle

- **Catch yourself**: Start noticing when you are critical of yourself. Is it when you look in the mirror, when you're at work, or when you forget something? Becoming aware of doing this is the first step to changing your story.
- **Challenge the critic**: For every negative thought, challenge it. If your inner voice says, "You're a failure," counter that with, "I'm doing my best, and that's enough." Challenge negative self-talk by asking, "Would I say this to someone I love?" If the answer is no, seek a kinder alternative.
- **Compassion over criticism**: Replace critical thoughts with compassionate ones. Instead of "I can't do anything right," try saying, "I'm learning and growing every day." Let your inner voice declare,

"I've got this". On the hard days, cut yourself some slack. Know that setbacks do not define you and that tomorrow will be better than today.
- **Mindful self-compassion pauses**: Take moments to check in with yourself throughout your day. Place a hand over your heart and ask, "What do I need right now?" It could be a break, a kind word, or a glass of water. Remember that when you are feeling thirsty, you are already dehydrated.
- **Self-compassion**: Dedicate a notebook to self-compassion. Each night, write down three kind things about yourself, three things you did well that day, or three things you can do to make tomorrow a better day.

REBUILDING SELF-ESTEEM WITH AFFIRMATIONS AND SETTING GOALS

Enduring a toxic relationship has a profound way of shackling one's self-esteem and often leaves some deep-rooted scars and beliefs that hide in your subconscious. The abuse creates doubt, fear, and worthlessness around one's self-perception. You may be reluctant to trust yourself, have a persistent fear of making mistakes, or hear a voice inside that constantly minimizes your achievements and worth, devaluing who you truly are. Recognizing how this harmful relationship skewed how you view yourself is crucial. Acknowledging the erosion of your self-esteem is a big step towards mending the cracks and rediscovering your inner strength and value.

Affirmations and positive self-talk remind you of your worth, capabilities, courage, and strength. Words have the power to heal or hurt, and in the aftermath of an abusive relationship, speaking kindly towards yourself is soothing the parts of you that have been deeply hurt.

Craft personal affirmations that resonate with your core truths. Phrases like "I deserve love and respect," "I am strong," or "I trust my intuition" can be incredibly empowering. Dedicate time each day to repeat your affirmations. Create morning and evening routines. Any moments of self-doubt necessitate an immediate affirmation to restate your inherent value.

Restoring your confidence grows as you progress. Setting and achieving small, manageable goals acts as proof of your capabilities, helping to reverse the negative narrative of worthlessness that was created by emotional abuse. Begin with goals that feel achievable and meaningful. Completing a daily walk, reading a book, or even organizing a space in your home can be significant goals.

Goals give us direction, but the key to making them impactful is to ensure they are SMART goals. Use this acronym, SMART, to help you ensure that your goals are something that you can accomplish. Specific, Measurable, Achievable, Relevant, and Time-bound. This framework can help you create clear, attainable goals. Be specific in what you want. Your goal should be measurable in a timeline and relevant to where you are in life.

This could mean breaking down your goal into smaller, achievable steps that you can track easily. Notice the difference between saying, "I want to be happier" and "I will dedicate ten minutes every morning to meditate for self-reflection." The latter is specific and measurable, providing a clear path and a straightforward way to celebrate when you achieve it. Use a journal to track your goals and progress. This becomes a motivational tool and a visual reminder of how far you've come. Celebrate each achievement, no matter how small, recognizing it as proof of your resilience and determination to regain your self-esteem.

PRIORITIZING YOUR PHYSICAL HEALTH

Prioritize activities that enhance your physical well-being, such as exercise, nutritious eating, getting adequate sleep, and engaging in activities that bring you happiness and peace. Listen to your body. It will signal what it needs: rest, movement, or nourishment. Pay attention to these signals, adjusting your self-care practices to meet your body's demands. Nurturing your body is like tending to the most visible part of your garden.

When the body is cared for, it becomes a strong vessel that carries you through any difficult times with ease. The basis of self-care is healthy eating with balanced meals, staying hydrated, regular exercise, and receiving any necessary medical care. Doing this shows that you are respecting your physical form, your body, that supports you every day.

Nutrition: Choose foods that fuel your body and mind. Incorporate healthy foods, including fruits and vegetables, lean proteins, and whole grains, that are packed with the nutrients necessary for energy and mental clarity. Focus on a diverse, healthy diet. This includes salmon, avocados, flax and chia seeds, sweet potatoes, blueberries, yogurt, green tea, chickpeas, dark, leafy green like spinach, and kale, to name a few. Be mindful of your salt intake. Excessive amounts are harmful to you. Avoid sugary food items. They may taste good, but sugar can cause mood swings and irritability. It gives you a high, followed by a low, and a craving for more. Find the superfoods that you would find enjoyable to eat. Dark chocolate provides a treat. Nourishing your body with balanced, wholesome meals provides you with what you need to navigate the emotional complexities of healing.

Exercise: Find a physical activity you enjoy. It could be bike riding, jogging, yoga, walking, or dancing. Often, when we feel thirsty, our body is already dehydrated. Have a water bottle with you to replenish any lost fluids. When you realize that regular movement releases endorphins, the body's natural stress relievers, you will be motivated to continue your activities. Exercise strengthens your body. Activities like yoga keep your body flexible. If you have an animal companion, notice how often they stretch when they get up. Make a habit of stretching frequently. Let these routines become a special part of your day, a time reserved for self-renewal just for you. Embrace flexibility in your routine, allowing it to evolve as you do. Identify which activities replenish your energy and incorporate them into your daily and weekly schedule.

Medical Care: Keep up with medical appointments. Don't ignore symptoms. Your physical well-being is crucial during this transformative time, and addressing any health concerns promptly ensures you remain strong and capable. Have a complete physical and dental check-up at least once a year. Many times, there are no symptoms of conditions like high blood pressure, glaucoma, and diabetes. Taking care of your physical body is a way to show that you value yourself. Make yourself your top priority.

EMOTIONAL AND MENTAL SELF-CARE

The heart and mind often bear the brunt of emotional turmoil and need tender care. As you navigate this time of significant change, remember that self-care is not a luxury but a necessity—this gentle care and attention you give yourself that paves the way for healing and growth. Finding joy and peace can seem like searching for a proverbial needle in a haystack. Yet, these bits of happiness form a buffer against the world's harshness. Here are some ways to cultivate self-care.

- **Emotional care**: Allow yourself to feel and express a range of emotions. Emotions come up to be released, not relived. Writing, talking with trusted friends, journaling, meditation, or any creative outlet can help you express and process emotions. If you are feeling an emotion that you don't understand, stop and ask, "Where is this coming from?"
- **Connection**: Connect with people who lift you up. Laughter and heartfelt conversations with friends can be incredibly healing, reminding you of joy and lightness. Engaging in activities that lift your spirit is a form of emotional self-care. Whether painting, gardening, or reading, hobbies provide an escape, a moment of joy amidst the chaos.
- **Mindful moments**: Seek out moments of mindfulness throughout your day. This could be savoring a cup of tea, feeling the sun on your face, or listening to a favorite piece of music. Engage your senses. Each mindful moment brings you a step toward inner peace.

- **Art therapy:** Engaging in creative endeavors can act as a form of therapy, allowing emotions to flow and be processed constructively. Creativity can boost self-esteem, providing a sense of achievement and purpose. Artistic expression offers a way to release pent-up emotions and facilitate a sense of relief. Focusing on a creative task can anchor you in the present moment, reducing anxiety, stress, and depression. It is a creative outlet that offers a sense of control and allows you to express yourself more freely.
- **Learn new skills**: Start small. A new skill doesn't necessarily mean something very challenging, like learning a new language. It could be preparing a meal you have never made before. Doing anything new can provide a sense of accomplishment and give a reprieve from temporary stressors.
- **Journaling**: Writing offers a private, unjudged space to spill your thoughts, fears, and hopes. It's a way to process feelings and make them less overwhelming. Reflect on and identify specific thoughts or beliefs about yourself that have affected and caused changes in your self-perception.
- **Meditation**: A few minutes a day can significantly improve your emotional well-being. Build slowly on this without judgment, and you will find that you can meditate more easily and for more extended periods of time. This practice helps center your thoughts and calm your mind.

THE MIND-BODY CONNECTION

Our thoughts and emotions directly affect our physical state. As you explore the mind-body connection, you discover more holistic ways to support your body and your mind. The stress and turmoil experienced both during and after leaving a toxic relationship can create physical symptoms like fatigue, insomnia, or a weakened immune system. There are healing methods that incorporate the mind and body with breathwork and understanding our energy. This energy goes by several different names depending on their point of origin from the cultures who spoke of it: prana, chi (pronounced chee), ki (pronounced key), and qi (also pronounced chee).

Working with this energy and connecting with your breath can significantly reduce stress and give you calm and clarity, supporting your emotional healing. Practices like yoga, meditation, and Qigong are ancient principles that can bring you back to a state of balance. They also provide physical benefits such as increased flexibility and strength, in addition to bringing you mental clarity and emotional equilibrium.

Meditation: It is a quieting practice that is a good way to begin or end your day. This becomes a grounding way to anchor you amidst any of life's upheavals. It is a time dedicated solely to your well-being, a space where your thoughts are quieted and a mind-body connection is encouraged. People can become discouraged and say they can't quiet their minds. Meditating and quieting your mind may seem impossible. Recognize that this thought can cause you to judge yourself and want to give up trying.

Meditation does take practice. We do have busy minds. One way to begin is to focus on your breath and notice how it fills your lungs. Direct your breath to where you want it to go. Visualize your lungs in the rib cage and slowly and deliberately fill them from the bottom to the top. Pay attention to how your abdomen rises with the breath and lowers with the exhale. This has a soothing and calming effect and will quiet the mind. The more often you do this, the easier it becomes. Trust that it is possible!

Yoga: This ancient practice combines physical postures, breath control, and meditation to enhance your overall well-being. Many people shy away from yoga, thinking they can't do the different poses. Yoga is adaptable and can be tailored to suit your physical capabilities and recovery needs. There are various types of yoga. There is Hatha yoga, vinyasa yoga, Bikram yoga, which is done in a heated room, Kundalini yoga, yin yoga, and restorative yoga, to name a few. Explore the ones that will work best for you because they are geared toward more specific needs.

Yoga gently builds muscle. At the end of a yoga practice, there will be a time to lie down and relax your body, known as savasana. Depending on the instructor, you are guided in a meditation or encouraged to do a full body scan from your toes to your head. This scan brings awareness to your body and the areas holding stress and allows you to release it. You can practice this on your own before going to sleep at night. Check your local gym for classes offered. Each time you do a yoga routine, it will become more familiar and comfortable, and you will notice the benefits you receive from it.

Qigong: This form of body movement allows you both serenity and connectedness with the Earth. It is deeply rooted in traditional Chinese medicine and brings you balance and harmony. The word Qigong loosely translates to cultivating life energy. No equipment is required as the poses are done in a standing position. You are guided to connect with your breath, with each posture, helping you to release and move energy. The movements are slow, gentle, and deliberate, fostering a connection to your body and the life force energy of the Universe. The gentle, controlled movements guide the chi, the universal life force energy, through your body, rejuvenating and recharging you. It is a great way to reduce tension and stress held within the body.

Check your local community college and high schools. Often, non-credit courses for these are offered in the evenings or on weekends at a very reasonable price. The library also frequently provides activities you can participate in. If you prefer to do this alone, there are many videos you can follow along in the privacy of your home.

Creating a routine that includes regular physical activity becomes a self-care ritual. In any form, exercise acts as a natural antidepressant and encourages the release of endorphins, which bolster mood and energy levels. It gives you focus, which helps you concentrate on what you need to do. Incorporating something you enjoy, like yoga or Qigong, transforms exercise from something unpleasant into a cherished part of your healing process.

HOLISTIC FORMS OF HEALING

The human body has the innate wisdom and ability to heal itself. However, stress or trauma can short-circuit and block this ability. By recognizing yourself as an energetic being, you understand that various healing energy modalities can assist you on a vibrational level. Energy healing is a holistic approach that acknowledges the interconnectedness of mind, body, and spirit, whether through hands-on or hands-off techniques. This approach can empower you, making you feel more in control of your health and connected with your soul.

Multiple practitioners have studied and learned how to connect and bring healing energy from the many non-traditional healing modalities to the Western world. Reiki, sound healing, acupuncture, inner child healing, and being the "hollow bone" are a few types of healing energy that I have either experienced or worked with. The term "hollow bone" refers to moving your ego to the side, asking for the highest and best to come through, and becoming a clear channel for this energy to flow. Any of these forms of healing therapy can stand alone or complement the more traditional therapy treatments:

Reiki is a holistic healing practice that originated in Japan in the early 20th century. It has gained global recognition and is now offered in various settings, including hospitals and nursing homes. The term 'Reiki' is derived from two Japanese words: 'rei,' meaning universal, and 'ki,' meaning life force energy. The practice is based on the belief that a practitioner channels this energy through their hands to bring healing and relaxation to the recipient. During a Reiki session, the practitioner places their hands lightly on or just above the individual's body. The recipient can choose to sit in a chair or lie on a table, and the practitioner focuses on the energy centers of the body known as the chakras. The practitioner is guided on where to place their hands and how long to stay in a specific area of the individual's body, ensuring a non-invasive and comfortable experience for the recipient.

Reiki helps to reduce stress and promote relaxation. By helping to balance the body's energy, Reiki can alleviate tension and anxiety, bringing a sense of calm and well-being. Many people also find that Reiki helps to relieve physical pain and discomfort. It is gentle and non-invasive and can be used as a complementary therapy alongside the more traditional treatments. As a Reiki practitioner, when I have given clients a session, they have said that they felt like other hands were bringing them energy in an area where I was not physically working. This, like many healing modalities, goes beyond the individual practitioner. The healing is not coming from the practitioner. It is coming through the practitioner. The practitioner becomes the vessel, the channel, that brings the energy through.

Sound healing is an ancient practice that understands the therapeutic properties of sound vibrations that promote healing and well-being in an individual or group of people. It includes various techniques, including singing bowls, tuning forks, drums, and vocal toning. To understand the benefits of this, we must realize that everything in the Universe, including our bodies, is in a state of vibration. We are energetic beings. When these vibrations, atoms, and molecules become out of harmony, we move into a state of imbalance.

During a sound healing session, the practitioner creates sounds and frequencies that resonate with the body's natural rhythmic vibrations, helping to restore balance and harmony. The vibrations produced by the sounds can penetrate deeply into the body, affecting cells, tissues, and organs at a cellular level. This process can help to release tension, reduce stress, and alleviate physical pain and discomfort. Sound healing promotes relaxation, enhances meditation, and facilitates emotional release and healing. The soothing sounds can quiet the mind, reduce anxiety and depression, and improve sleep quality. A certified sound healer has the knowledge and understanding of the ways to balance the chakras.

Acupuncture is a traditional Chinese medicine practice performed by a trained and licensed practitioner and is well-regarded for its holistic approach to health and well-being. Acupuncture has been used for thousands of years to treat a variety of conditions, including pain, stress, anxiety, and insomnia. This practice involves the insertion of thin needles into specific points on the body. These points, known as acupuncture points or acupoints, are located along pathways called meridians through which "qi" or vital energy flows. Blockages in the flow of qi can come from trauma or emotional issues. Acupuncture stimulates and balances the flow of this energy within the body to promote healing and restore health. Inserting thin needles, which are not painful, into specific acupoints helps to open the flow of energy, supporting the body's natural ability to heal itself.

INTEGRATING MINDFULNESS INTO DAILY LIFE

In our fast-paced world, our minds can sometimes resemble browser tabs all opened simultaneously, each vying for attention, making it hard to focus or even breathe. Mindfulness brings us back to the present, closing each tab until the only open one is in the present moment. In this state of awareness, we know where and what we are doing without being reactive or overwhelmed by what's happening around us. Mindfulness can calm the chaos of your daily life as you become more aware of your thoughts and feelings and learn to observe them without judgment. This awareness helps you manage your emotions more easily. This isn't about escaping reality. It is discovering an inner sanctuary where you can retreat, even if just for a moment, to regain clarity and peace. Throughout the day, take short breaks for breathing exercises. Close your eyes and focus on your breath, inhaling fully and slowly and exhaling just as slowly. Even a minute of focused breathing can center and calm your mind.

Mindfulness is something easily accessible. You do not need special equipment or a designated space to practice it. The practice offers a wealth of benefits. It enhances the quality of your life. As you brush your teeth or take your morning shower, focus on the sensations you feel, the taste of the toothpaste, or the sound of the water. These simple acts set a mindful tone for the day and enhance your ability to focus. Practicing mindfulness trains your brain to stay on task without getting easily distracted and improves concentration.

Pay close attention to the present moment, whether eating, walking, or breathing. Before eating, take a moment to appreciate the colors and smells of your food. Chew slowly, savoring each bite and paying attention to the taste and texture. Simple tasks become opportunities for self-awareness. Bringing your attention to the present stops you from overthinking or worrying about the future. Regular mindfulness practice can increase your resilience to the challenges that arise, making it easier to bounce back from any setbacks.

Incorporating mindfulness into your life starts with small moments, choosing to pause and breathe amid the daily rush. You give yourself permission to slow down and be present, recognizing that in this moment, you are enough and have enough. It becomes not just a practice but a way of life. It leads you to a more centered, peaceful existence, no matter the storms surrounding you.

NATURE HEALS THE BODY, MIND AND SOUL

Stepping into nature can be a transformative experience, whether it's a park, the beach, the forest, or even your backyard. Walking barefoot can create a profound connection with the Earth, nurturing your spiritual and emotional well-being. Nature can be a sanctuary during times of stress or grief, fostering feelings of gratitude, humility, and interconnectedness. It can inspire a deeper appreciation for the Earth's beauty and biodiversity, evoking a sense of reverence for the natural world.

Spending time outdoors can enhance your cognitive

function and encourage innovative thinking and imagination.

Breathing fresh air and being surrounded by greenery or water is a natural way to boost your health. Exposure to the natural environment has been shown to strengthen the immune system and increase resilience to illness. Connecting with nature soothes you and brings you to a place of calm. You will find peace, clarity, and a renewed sense of purpose here.

If you live in the city and finding a place in nature is a challenge, look at beautiful nature scenes to uplift you. Choose a stunning scene that has meaning to you, a place you've been to or would like to go. Hang it on a wall or set it as the background on your computer or cell phone. Seeing this will be a continuous reminder of the world's beauty and also becomes a goal for you to visit this area in the near future.

Use daily walks as a chance to practice mindfulness. Focus on the rhythm of your steps, the feel of the ground under your feet, and the sounds around you. Walk a little slower than usual. Notice the sensation as your foot connects with the Earth. If your mind wanders, gently bring your attention back to your walking. Doing this gives you a new connectedness to the Earth that you may not have had before.

IMPORTANCE OF RESTFUL SLEEP

Studies reveal that, on average, we need between 7 to 9 hours of sleep a night. These numbers will vary with individuals, with younger people needing more sleep than older adults. Getting a good night's sleep is crucial for your physical and emotional recovery and healthy functioning. Create a routine that signals to your body that it's time to wind down.

Engage in relaxing activities such as reading a book or a self-care routine, a bath, gentle stretching, or breathing exercises. Set up an environment conducive to your sleep needs, a comfortable temperature, and low light. Avoid caffeine, nicotine, and alcohol, which can make it more difficult to fall asleep and can also interfere with your sleep quality. If you live in a noisy area, consider getting noise-canceling headphones or listening to quiet, meditative music.

Research shows that the blue light from electronic devices can interfere with sleep by affecting the circadian rhythm or sleep cycle. This blue light signals your brain to wake up when it should be winding down. One study showed that as little as 2 hours of exposure to this light at night slowed or stopped the release of the sleep hormone melatonin. Avoid screen time for at least an hour before bed.

Exposure to natural light and fresh air during the day can help regulate the body's circadian rhythms and improve sleep quality. Spending time outdoors can promote relaxation and a sense of calm, leading to better sleep patterns and overall restorative rest. Allow yourself to do this guilt-free. Sleep is a vital part of the recovery process, and you may need more sleep than usual as you heal and reclaim all the parts of yourself that were lost from the toxic relationship.

REFLECTING

When you reflect, you view and examine experiences from a place of calm and clarity. You are being the observer, the witness rather than the reactor. Through reflection, you integrate your experiences, nurturing them as you work on becoming whole again. Journaling offers you a way to organize thoughts, feelings, and experiences and make sense of them in the context of your life. Writing is space for honesty, your dreams, and understanding who you are and aspire to be. Meditation clears the noise, bringing you into a state of quiet where insights can surface as you move to the depths within yourself.

Nurturing your emotional well-being supports your physical health. Incorporating practices like mindfulness, meditation, art therapy, or energy healing improves the benefits of the traditional therapeutic approaches. These offer a more comprehensive journey to wellness and provide you with a complete set of tools for healing and finding that state of balance and harmony within you.

Every step you take to prioritize yourself is a step towards a stronger, more resilient you. You heal on multiple levels as you reclaim your well-being, piece by piece, and honor the connection between your body and mind. This prepares you for the journey ahead, where you continue to explore, grow, and rediscover the depths of your strength and resilience.

> *Do not judge me by my success, judge me by how many times I fell down and got back up again.*
>
> — NELSON MANDELA

TRUSTING YOURSELF AND OTHERS

Trust is the foundation of any healthy relationship. Without it, love and respect cannot thrive.

— DAVID FOSTER WALLACE

After a toxic relationship, trust can be a challenge to rebuild, but it is essential for forming healthy connections and believing in yourself. The abuse from a manipulative relationship can make you second-guess yourself and leave you suspicious of other people's intentions. The idea of trusting again can feel almost impossible.

As you realize how the manipulation has changed your self-perception, desires, and needs, you must now regain trust in who you are and what you can do. The ability to trust, not just in others but also in yourself, is necessary for navigating new relationships with wisdom and confidence. The capacity to trust again exists inside your inner wounds of childhood neglect, betrayal, and hurtful relationships.

Imagine holding a piece of delicate, beautiful porcelain that has been shattered. At first glance, it seems irreparable. But with patience, the right tools, and a steady hand, those pieces can be put back together. Kintsugi is a Japanese word that means join with gold. It is the art of repairing a cherished vessel and sealing the seams with lacquer mixed with gold or silver powder. The mended breaks become part of the beauty. You may still notice where the breaks were, but this vessel can still function and hold its beauty. This is a metaphor to help you see the beauty and stay optimistic when things seem to fall apart and to help rebuild the trust that has been broken by experiencing a toxic relationship.

BUILDING TRUST SLOWLY

The key is to take time with new connections and understand and address the trust issues head-on. It starts with acknowledging the hurt and recognizing that while the past has shaped you, it doesn't define your future interactions. When you learn to trust yourself, you also learn to respect yourself and your abilities.

Rome wasn't built in a day, and neither is trust. It is constructed brick by brick, with each interaction adding to the foundation. When forming new relationships, setting a pace that feels comfortable for you is of utmost importance.

- **Communicate at your pace**: Letting people know you prefer to take things slow is not a sign of weakness but of self-awareness. It sets the tone for

the relationship, ensuring that your boundaries are respected.
- **Incremental sharing**: You do not have to share your deepest fears or secrets to test the waters of trust. Start by sharing small, less personal stories or opinions and gauge the reaction. This is a way to observe how respectful and understanding the other person is to you and your needs.
- **Celebrate small victories**: Every time someone respects your pace or a boundary, it's a small victory. Acknowledge these moments, as they reinforce the trust-building process.

Start with small acts of trust in yourself and others. Each time your trust is respected, you take another step toward rebuilding this crucial foundation. To truly thrive as you move on requires support, resilience, and renewed trust. Remember, for every person who has hurt you, there are many more people who want to help you. Your goal is to let this help come into your life. Begin with small steps.

- **Trust-building activities**: Engage in activities that require trust but within a safe context. Group sports, workshops, or team-building exercises can be great for this. Joining a book club can give you a place to safely speak and share your opinions.
- **Seeking therapy and support groups**: Sometimes, an outside perspective can make a world of difference. Therapists or support group members can provide insights into why trust is challenging for you and offer strategies to gradually rebuild it.

PAYING ATTENTION TO YOUR INNATE GIFTS

Your intuition and your gut feelings are two powerful tools. Your intuition is that inner voice that whispers truths that you need to face. It could be a gentle nudge to go in a specific direction. Trusting this instinct is crucial when navigating away from toxic dynamics. Your intuition is a guide that can lead you towards trustworthy people and away from those who may harm you.

Your gut can signal when boundaries are being crossed or when interactions leave you drained rather than uplifted. If something feels wrong, it most likely is. Your gut feeling is an invaluable compass when navigating new relationships. It is that feeling or sometimes a loud alarm signaling to avoid a particular person or situation. Spotting red flags early on can help you avoid potential repeat circumstances. Tune into behaviors that made you uncomfortable in the past and be mindful of them with new acquaintances.

Honoring these inherent tools and not rationalizing these feelings away protects your well-being. Trusting them helps you walk away from circumstances or individuals that make you uneasy without needing a logical explanation. Let your intuition and gut guide you toward healthy, fulfilling relationships rooted in mutual respect. These exercises help connect you with your intuition:

- **Mindfulness practices**: Mindfulness can sharpen your intuition and inner knowing. Meditation or quiet contemplation can help you tune into your inner voice. Focusing on your breath quiets the

chatter that often occupies the mind and allows you to feel calm and centered.
- **Journaling**: Keep track of the times when you listened to your intuition or your gut and found it accurate. Also, recall when you ignored these feelings and wished you hadn't. This can be eye-opening, providing a clear view of your inner wisdom and the proof you need to trust it.

HEALTHY RELATIONSHIP INDICATORS

Recognizing the signs of a healthy relationship can guide you toward connections that are nurturing and supportive. These indicators act as beacons, lighting the path to trust and mutual respect.

- **Consistent respect**: Look for consistency in how you are treated. Respect should be a constant, not something that fluctuates based on circumstances.
- **Open communication**: Healthy relationships thrive on open, honest communication. Whether discussing a difficult topic or sharing joy, both should feel safe and natural.
- **Mutual support**: A healthy relationship is built on mutual support for each other's goals, dreams, and personal growth. It is about lifting each other, not holding one another back.

Once trust has been broken, rebuilding it requires both time and patience with yourself. Allow it to happen at a pace that honors your experiences and respects your growth. In navigating new relationships with confidence and clarity, draw upon the skills you have developed of honest communication, understanding yourself, and connecting with your intuition. These tools guide you in forming meaningful connections and enriching your journey.

A phrase from a poem written by Brian A. Chalker states people come into your life for a reason, a season, or a lifetime. Approach each new friendship with an open heart and no expectations of the reason. Realize that it is all part of your journey. As you move forward, remember these words as you create bonds with others who will be there to help you or enrich your life in some way.

THE POWER OF FORGIVENESS: LETTING GO OF BITTERNESS

> *To forgive is to set a prisoner free and to discover the prisoner was you.*
>
> — CORRIE TEN BOOM

Forgiveness can often seem out of reach, especially for a deep hurt. At its core, forgiveness is setting down a heavy load you have been carrying, not for the benefit of the person who wronged you but for your own peace. It's an act of self-care. It is a silent declaration that your well-being is paramount and that you are no longer willing to let past hurts dictate your emotional state.

Holding onto anger and bitterness is like drinking poison and waiting for the other person to suffer. It consumes your thoughts, colors your perceptions, and can even manifest in physical symptoms. Letting go of these toxic emotions frees up space in your heart and mind for more constructive, life-affirming feelings. Choose not to let someone else's actions continue to have power over your happiness and peace of mind. Embarking on the path to forgiveness involves several significant steps:

- **Acknowledging the pain**: The first step is admitting to yourself that you were hurt. Trying to downplay the pain or brush it aside only delays healing. Recognizing and acknowledging that someone's actions caused you pain is not a sign of weakness. It allows for the healing to begin.
- **Understanding the impact**: Reflect on how holding onto this anger has affected you. Has it changed how you interact with others? Has it influenced your view of yourself? Understanding these impacts can be a powerful motivator in your decision to let go.
- **Making a conscious choice to forgive**: Forgiveness is a decision to accept and move on. It is not a one-time action but a choice you may need to reaffirm, especially on difficult days.

Forgiving yourself, especially for staying in a toxic relationship, is equally crucial. It's easy to fall into a cycle of self-blame, to berate yourself for not seeing the signs or leaving sooner. Yet, reprimanding yourself serves no purpose. It will only prolong your pain. Recognize that you did your best with what you had at the time.

- **Seeing the lessons**: Every experience, no matter how painful, has something to teach us. It may have taught you about your strength and resilience or even clarified what you truly value in relationships. Recognizing the lesson was a way to uncover the reason, to see it as something that, while it may have brought you low, also showed you just how strong you can be. Life lessons are valuable for your growth and evolution.

- **Practicing self-compassion**: Be as kind to yourself as you would be to a friend in a similar situation. Remind yourself that everyone makes mistakes, and you deserve happiness and love as much as anyone else.
- **Mantra**: It is very healing to repeat this affirmation: "I forgive myself. I forgive all others. I am completely forgiven. I forgive the past and I embrace a future that is filled with hope, love and infinite possibilities." Words spoken out loud move from the conscious mind to the subconscious. Healing happens on many different levels. The layers of the subconscious run so deep. It can be ingrained with thoughts that you are not even aware of. Beliefs can go beyond this life's experience and be held within our ancestral DNA. This is why we say, I forgive it all. We are forgiving lifetimes of hardship.

When you incorporate forgiveness into your life, you are not condoning what happened to you or forgetting it. You are choosing not to let it define you or your future, and you are no longer defined by the hurts you have experienced. It is a powerful act of reclaiming your narrative as you choose healing and peace over resentment and pain. This is your declaration of independence from the past and a commitment to your emotional and mental well-being.

CULTIVATING SELF-RESPECT: DAILY PRACTICES FOR EVERYDAY LIFE

Self-respect is a mirror that reflects our deepest values and beliefs back at us. This is more than feeling good about yourself, it's about recognizing your worth through the actions and decisions that align with your core values. Cultivating self-respect ensures that each day contributes to a more confident, assertive, and independent you.

Incorporating rituals that affirm your self-respect into your daily routine can transform the mundane into moments of empowerment. These rituals serve as constant reminders of your value, reinforcing the commitment to treat yourself with kindness and understanding.

- **Morning affirmations**: Start the day by stating affirmations that resonate with your self-worth. Stand in front of the mirror, stating your strengths and commitment to honoring your needs and boundaries. Speak with authority and purpose.
- **Mindful reflection**: Dedicate a few minutes each evening to reflect on the day. Ask yourself how you honored your worth and where you might have compromised. Use this time to reaffirm your commitment to self-respect.
- **Self-care routines**: Plan self-care into your daily activities. Whether you choose nutritious food, engage in physical activity, or set aside time for hobbies that nourish your soul, make self-care an unbreakable part of your routine.

Boundaries as Self-Respect

Setting and maintaining boundaries is the most tangible expression of self-respect. Doing this declares that you value your well-being and peace of mind above pleasing other people. Boundaries are not barriers but the explicit expression of how you expect to be treated based on your self-worth. Clearly define your limits and what you will accept in your interactions and relationships.

In bringing self-respect into your daily life, you honor your worth and teach others how to treat you. From the rituals that start and end your day to how you assert your needs and defend your boundaries, each action builds a protective layer to preserve your peace and dignity. Remember, self-respect isn't inherited or bestowed—it's cultivated through consistent practice and reaffirming your intrinsic value. You may still occasionally have to speak up if your boundaries are crossed and point out why it is important to you. Each time you do this, you reconfirm your self-worth.

THE SIGNIFICANCE OF COMMUNITY

Creating a life that meets its fullest potential often begins with finding the connections that bring shared joy. Discovering your tribe or community is like being in a garden where you can contribute and reap the benefits of collective growth and happiness. This process involves seeking those who share your interests and finding places where you feel a sense of belonging and support.

The quest for joy often leads us to seek new avenues to explore and engage in activities that light up our world. In these pursuits, whether art, music, sports, or any other passion, we find others who resonate with our excitement and enthusiasm. This shared vibrancy becomes the cornerstone of forming a community that uplifts its members.

- **Start by listing activities** that make you lose track of time, those that fill you with energy and happiness.
- **Look for local clubs,** online groups, or community classes where these activities are celebrated. These are potential spots to meet like-minded individuals.
- **Remember,** the goal is to enrich your life with connections and experiences that bring you joy.

Stepping out of your comfort zone is a big step in personal growth. You are opening doors to new communities and sources of joy. As you dare to try new things, you signal to yourself and the world that you value your happiness and are open to the adventures waiting to be explored.

- **Embrace the unfamiliar with enthusiasm**: Every new activity, whether a cooking class, a hiking group, or a book club, contributes to your connectedness to your community.
- **Celebrate your growth**: Remember that each success, no matter how small, builds self-worth and reminds you of what you can achieve.

Active participation in your community enhances your sense of belonging and reinforces your role as a valuable member of a collective. Sharing your skills, time, or even enthusiasm for a cause or activity contributes to the community's vibrancy and, in return, feeds your soul with joy and fulfillment. Volunteer for roles that align with your interests and strengths. It could be organizing events, leading activities, or simply being a supportive member. As you notice the positive impact of your contributions, you develop a sense of accomplishment and connection.

The communities we build and engage with reflect the journey taken toward finding joy and regaining self-worth. They remind us that while the path to rediscovering ourselves might be personal, we don't have to walk it alone. The shared laughter, support, and connections we foster enrich us to a fuller, happier life. Our strength is amplified by the bonds we make and the friendships we nurture.

Acknowledgment, support, forgiveness, and self-care are pillars of rebuilding your life. They pave the way for a future where relationships are sources of joy and growth, not pain and restriction. With these foundations in place, you are ready to move ahead.

Have enough courage to trust love one more time and always one more time.

— MAYA ANGELOU

Part Four
EMBRACING LIFE

RECLAIMING YOUR ESSENCE AND BELIEVING IN YOURSELF

When you find love, you will find yourself. When you have the knowledge of love, you will then feel peace in your heart. Stop searching here and there, the Jewels are inside you. This, my friend, is the holy meaning of love.

— RUMI

Visualize standing in front of a mirror, not to criticize or to admire, but to see yourself for the first time. This reflection holds the experiences, beliefs, and values that shape who you are. This moment is an intimate encounter with your core essence. Here, in this quiet introspection, lies the foundation of self-worth. This is not only feeling good about yourself but recognizing and embracing your intrinsic value of achievements and resilience.

In this chapter, we will explore how what we value will renew our sense of self-worth. Our values move us toward actions and decisions that align with who we truly are. When we live in harmony with these values, our self-worth flourishes, painting our world with vibrant authenticity and respect.

IDENTIFYING PERSONAL VALUES

Values are your internal GPS, guiding you through life's many choices and challenges. Pinpointing these values requires a deep dive into your inner world. Meditation is a powerful tool in this exploration, allowing you to peel back the layers of perceived expectations through your personal experiences and allowing you to uncover your true self.

Set aside time each day for quiet reflection. Make this a habit and choose a specific time, either first thing in the morning or before bedtime. Use guided meditations available through apps or online platforms, focusing on self-discovery meditations. Choose the meditation that offers you the contemplation you need as you do your soul-searching. Ask yourself key questions during meditation, like "What moments bring me the most joy?" or "When do I feel most like myself?" Explore the many meditations available on YouTube. Doing these exercises will help you notice patterns and themes, pointing you toward your core values.

The link between understanding your values and developing self-worth is undeniable. When you act in ways that align with your values, you send a powerful message of your self-respect and integrity. Each time you make a decision based on your values, you affirm your worth and reinforce your esteem. For example, if honesty is a core value, you strengthen your self-worth each time you choose transparency over convenience. Consistent actions grounded in your values create the base for your self-esteem. By anchoring yourself to these values, you are able to navigate life's tumultuous waters with confidence and grace.

Living in alignment with your values can be challenging, especially when faced with pressure to conform to external expectations. Your true worth is not determined by external influences but by what you cherish and who you are as a person. Here are some strategies to connect to your values:

- **Write down your top five values** and keep them where you can see them daily. This constant reminder helps to guide your decisions.
- **Set boundaries** that protect your ability to live according to your values and prioritize what is most important to you.
- **Reflect regularly** on your actions and decisions. Ask yourself if they reflect your values and how they contribute to your sense of worthiness.

EMBRACING SOLITUDE: FINDING PEACE IN BEING ALONE

In a world that often equates being alone with loneliness, discovering the true essence of solitude can transform our relationship with ourselves. Solitude, when approached with intention and openness, becomes a canvas on which we paint our deepest thoughts, fears, and dreams. It offers a rare pause in life's relentless pace, a space to breathe, reflect, and grow.

To see solitude as an ally rather than an adversary requires a shift in perspective. Imagine solitude not as an empty room but as a garden where the seeds of self-awareness and peace can flourish. In these quiet moments, you can listen to your inner voice, understand your desires, and tune in to what makes you truly happy. This understanding fosters a profound connection with yourself, laying the groundwork for a relationship rooted in respect and affection.

Solo Activities for Healing

Engaging in activities alone can be soothing and a bridge to deeper self-understanding. Consider these pursuits not just as pastimes but as rituals of self-care:

- **Nature walks**: Wander through nature, observe the intricate details of the world around you, and find a rhythm in your steps that matches the beat of your heart.
- **Reading**: Lose yourself in stories and ideas that challenge, inspire, and comfort you. Let each book be a doorway to new worlds and perspectives.
- **Creative pursuits**: Whether painting, writing, or playing music, creative activities allow you to express emotions that words alone cannot capture.

Benefits of Journaling

Journaling stands out as a powerful tool for self-discovery and healing. It acts as a mirror, reflecting your innermost thoughts and feelings back to you. Putting pen to paper helps untangle the web of emotions, offering clarity and insight. As you jot down your thoughts, you will find that journaling can:

- **Serve as an emotional release**, allowing you to express feelings in a safe, private space.

- **Help clarify your thoughts**, making it easier to understand complex emotions and situations.
- **Offers a record** of your progress over time, showing you how far you have come on your path to healing, and reflect on the progress.

Using journaling as a way to track your healing journey can reveal the subtle shifts in your mindset and emotional state over time. Look back on your entries from weeks or months ago and notice:

- How your perception of certain events or feelings has evolved.
- The growth in your understanding of yourself and your needs.
- The changes in how you respond to challenges or setbacks.

This reflection underscores the progress you've made, reinforcing the value of your solitude and the work you've done to heal and grow.

Building a Relationship with Oneself

At the heart of solitude is the opportunity to build a relationship with oneself that is as nurturing, supportive, and loving as those we seek with others. This relationship becomes the foundation upon which our self-worth is built. To foster this connection:

- Practice self-dialogue that is kind and compassionate. Speak to yourself as you would to a dear friend.

- Dedicate time to activities that fulfill you, recognizing these moments as acts of self-love.
- Acknowledge your needs, desires, and feelings as valid and important, worthy of attention and care.

The Power of Silence

In the quiet of solitude, silence becomes not just the absence of noise but a presence filled with potential for growth and introspection. Embracing silence allows you to:

- Hear the voice of your intuition, guiding you towards your truth and authenticity.
- Find peace in the simplicity of the state of being rather than doing.
- Connect with the profound depths of your inner world, discovering joys and sorrows previously drowned out by the clamor of daily life.

Solitude, with its quiet strength and gentle revelations, offers a path to self-discovery that is both profound and liberating. In the stillness, we find not loneliness but a companion in ourselves, someone ready to walk with us through life's ups and downs.

By doing activities that nourish your soul, journaling to clarify your thoughts, and reflecting on moments that highlight your growth, you cultivate a relationship with yourself based on love and respect. In the embrace of silence, you uncover the peace and wisdom that have been within you all along.

POSITIVE AFFIRMATIONS FOR BUILDING CONFIDENCE

In the quiet moments of self-reflection, we often encounter a chorus of doubts whispering their limitations into our thoughts. These are the times when the power of positive affirmations becomes a beacon of light, guiding us back to our inherent worth and potential.

The art of creating personal affirmations involves more than stringing together positive words. They are choosing phrases that resonate deeply with your innermost desires and truths. List qualities you would like to emanate. Reflect on the attributes or achievements that fill you with pride. Identify what lights up your soul.

From this list, write affirmations that reverberate these thoughts holding these qualities and goals. For instance, if you seek to cultivate inner peace, say the affirmation, "With each breath, I invite peace into my being." Speak affirmations out loud to reinforce them in your subconscious mind. Keep each affirmation in the present tense, as if it already exists in your reality.

Implementing Affirmations

Integrating affirmations into your daily life can transform them from mere words into your life's truths. Set specific times throughout the day for your affirmation practice. Aim for the morning as you welcome the day and the evening as you reflect. These are potent times to do this. Write your affirmations on sticky notes and put them where you will see them regularly—on your bathroom mirror, computer monitor, or refrigerator. Every time you repeat an affirmation, say it with intention, visualizing it as your reality. This practice is more than recitation; it's embodying the essence of your words.

Consider using mala beads, which typically have 108 beads, to make your positive affirmations. Moving the beads through your fingers one at a time as you breathe deliberately and slowly relaxes your central nervous system. The action of your fingers touching the beads brings sensory information to your brain, calming it. When using the mala beads, you can recite any number of different intentions. For example, you can say 12 intentions nine times each or any other various multiples you choose. You can record these affirmations on your cellphone for the days you feel tired and then listen to them as you move each bead through your fingers. Repeating affirmations multiple times reinforces the intention.

Affirmations as a Tool for Change

Positive affirmations are a powerful catalyst for altering negative thought patterns that undermine your confidence. When faced with self-doubt or criticism, counter it with an affirmation that champions your worth and capabilities. This practice does more than offer a moment of upliftment; it gradually rewires your brain. Regular affirmation practice can shift your focus from perceived limitations to your strengths and potential, creating a mindset where possibilities expand and barriers recede.

Research indicates that positive affirmations can bolster confidence and well-being. One study found that individuals who practiced self-affirmations were more likely to view threats or challenges as opportunities for growth. Other research highlighted how affirmations can reduce stress and improve problem-solving while under pressure. These findings validate the power of affirmations and illuminate their role in nurturing and creating a resilient, confident self.

As you add affirmations into your daily routines, remember that each positive statement is a step towards silencing doubts and awakening to your full potential. Through crafting, implementing, and believing in the power of your affirmations, you pave the way for a life where confidence blooms, unfettered by any doubts of insecurity.

THE TRANSFORMATIONAL SHIFT OF GRATITUDE

Studies show gratitude's profound impact on our mental and physical health. Gratitude, with its roots deep in our psyche, can transform our outlook on life, fostering a sense of contentment and well-being. It strengthens our immune system, lowers stress levels, and enhances sleep quality. These benefits are documented in many scientific journals and emphasize that gratitude is a catalyst for mental health and personal growth. Being grateful helps challenges transform into opportunities and hardships into lessons.

- **Practicing daily gratitude**: Take a moment to reflect on things you are grateful for each day. This simple practice can shift your focus from what is lacking to the abundance that is present in your life. It could be something as simple as a soft, lush bath towel or an uplifting experience that happened to you during the day.
- **Gratitude journal**: Keep a dedicated journal for jotting down thoughts of gratitude. Over time, this

record becomes a testament to the positive aspects of your life and a reminder during times of doubt or distress.

Gratitude for what we have accomplished and appreciation for the value we have created in our lives significantly enhances our relationship with the world. By noticing and focusing on the positive aspects of our interactions and expressing genuine appreciation for the people we connect with, we cultivate an environment of mutual respect, affection, and true friendship.

- **Acknowledge small acts of kindness**: A simple 'thank you' can go a long way in acknowledging others' efforts and fostering a positive dynamic.
- **Reflect on positive interactions**: At the end of each day, reflect on your interactions and find moments you are grateful for. This practice not only bolsters your mood but also reinforces the value of your connections.

YOUR PERSONAL DEFINITION OF SUCCESS

In this world that often measures worth by outer achievements, there is something revolutionary about crafting your definition of success. This becomes the quiet rebellion against the noise of society's expectations, a reclaiming of your narrative. Here, success isn't a one-size-fits-all but a profoundly individual elaboration of what truly matters to you. Put aside what is defined as benchmarks of success—wealth, status, possessions—and turn inward. Ask yourself, "What does success feel like to me?" Is it the freedom to pursue your passions, the strength of your relationships, or the personal growth you experience?

Pinpointing what success means to you lights your path, guiding you in the direction you want to go. Contemplate and reflect on moments you have felt truly fulfilled. What elements were present? Your joy, peace, and growth become part of the equation for your definition of success.

In the journey toward redefined success, every achievement, no matter its size, deserves recognition. Celebrating these milestones nurtures your self-worth, reclaims your value, and reinforces your dedicated commitment to your path. You move forward in your life with the understanding that success is not a destination but a series of meaningful, empowering experiences that reflect your hard work and show everything you have accomplished.

When you have exhausted all possibilities, remember this: you haven't.

— THOMAS A. EDISON

BEGIN THRIVING, CREATING YOUR FUTURE

Set your life on fire. Seek those who fan your flame.

— RUMI

Imagine you are standing at the edge of a vast landscape. Behind you lies a terrain marked by the remnants of the battles fought and the victories won. Ahead of you, the horizon stretches wide, a blank canvas, full of possibilities. This moment begins the path you forge as you move forward. Take a deep healing breath, and decide where you want to go and who you want to be when you get there.

As we walk the path, we find amongst the obstacles that we navigate, there are hidden treasures along the way. Remember that the path from healing to thriving is as unique as you are. There's no right or wrong way to proceed, only your way. With vision, goals, and all that you have learned at your disposal, you are well-equipped to turn your vision into a reality. Have a destination in mind, but the journey is where the magic happens. Before you can set any goals, have a clear picture of what you're aiming for. Envision what you want your future to look like and let yourself dream big.

GOAL-SETTING STRATEGIES ALIGNED WITH YOUR VALUES

When you understand your values, setting goals becomes an exercise in alignment rather than aspiration. These goals act as stepping stones toward the success you envision. If creativity is a core value, success might mean dedicating time daily to your art, not necessarily achieving recognition for it. Knowing what you value ensures that each goal met is a genuine step toward your happiness. List your core values and consider how they translate into personal and professional goals, focusing on the process as much as the outcome.

Creating a vision board is an excellent way to bring your vision to life. It's a visual representation of what you want to achieve. Use magazine cutouts, drawings, or any visuals that resonate with the life you imagine. Place it somewhere you will see daily as a constant reminder of your aspirations. Let your vision board be filled with everything you want to experience in life. Ask yourself: What does a fulfilling life look like to me? What am I passionate about? What have I always dreamed of doing but never pursued?

Mind mapping is a great tool to plan your future goals. It helps you organize your thoughts, prioritize your actions, and make your dreams more concrete. Start with a main focal point. Jot down all the things that make you feel alive. Use keywords, phrases, or images to represent your ideas.

Your map can be continuously revised, expanded, and refined as new ideas emerge and as you continue to grow. Mind mapping can help you see connections between different aspects of your life and identify areas where you want to put more time, money, and energy.

With your vision in hand, it is time to break it down into actionable goals. The aim here is progress, not perfection. Remember to set goals that are Specific, Measurable, Achievable, Relevant, and Time-bound (SMART). Tackling too much at once can be overwhelming, so start in increments that you can handle. Break your goals down into smaller steps that are manageable. For example, if you dream of running a marathon, start by committing to a regular running schedule and increase the distance you cover as you progressively get stronger.

THE JOURNEY OF GROWTH

Recognize that growth is an ongoing process. You'll likely encounter detours and roadblocks and sometimes need to reroute your path. This is all part of the adventure. The key is to remain flexible and adapt to change as it comes.

- **Reflect regularly**: Set aside time each week to reflect on your progress. Consider what's working, what isn't, and how you might need to adjust your approach.
- **Stay open to learning**: Embrace new experiences and challenges as opportunities to learn and grow. Whether it's picking up a new skill or tackling a fear, every step forward is a victory.

- **Celebrate milestones**: Always acknowledge your achievements along the way by doing something to recognize them. Continue to talk to your inner child, letting them know that they are always being heard and supported.

ADAPTING AND EMBRACING CHANGE

Change is inevitable and shapes the contours of our lives, transforming what is familiar into new possibilities. It is the only constant, a truth as old as time. There are times, though, that this can still be unsettling. Recognizing change as a natural force in life paves the way to embrace growth and renewal. It prompts you to adapt, to reassess your path, and sometimes, to forge a new one entirely. Viewing change through a lens of positivity allows you to extract valuable lessons from each twist and turn. It shows you that you can weather storms and emerge stronger on the other side. To embrace change effectively:

- **Stay present**: Focus on the here and now, acknowledging your feelings without becoming overwhelmed by them. This mindfulness helps you navigate change with a clearer head and a steadier heart.
- **Look for the lesson**: Every change brings another lesson to learn. By seeking out these hidden nuggets of wisdom, you transform change from something to endure into something to celebrate. Take the notion that things happen for you, not to you.

Change brings beauty and challenges, just like the change of seasons. Accepting change as an integral part of existence allows you to view it not as a disruptor but as a catalyst for personal evolution. This is the force that propels you from stagnation to action, urging you to explore beyond your comfort zones. When you see change as an opportunity rather than a threat, you open yourself to the richness of experience it brings.

Adaptability is a strength, like water—fluid, resilient, and capable of carving canyons out of solid rock. Developing adaptability involves sharpening your skills that allow you to navigate life's unpredictable tides with poise, ease and grace.

- **Flexibility**: Like the branches of the trees swaying in the wind, flexibility is about bending without breaking. It's finding alternative paths to our goals when obstacles arise. Always remain receptive to new ideas and approaches.
- **Openness**: Keeping an open mind is essential for adaptability. Be willing to explore new perspectives and consider different solutions. Cultivating curiosity and a love for learning new things keeps the mind nimble and ready for change.
- **Resilience**: Resilience is our emotional buoyancy, which allows us to bounce back from setbacks with renewed vigor. Building resilience involves cultivating a positive outlook, practicing self-care, and learning from each experience while embracing the challenge.

Change happens with life transitions, whether chosen or thrust upon us. They are pivotal moments that can redefine our path. Moving through these transitions with confidence requires a blend of self-awareness and strategy. Each new phase in your life can trigger a painful moment in time that still needs to be healed.

- **Self-reflection**: Regular self-reflection helps us understand our reactions to change and identify what we need to move forward. Check in with yourself, acknowledge your feelings, and assess your strengths and areas for growth.
- **Planning**: While we cannot plan for every eventuality, having a flexible plan in place can provide a sense of direction during times of transition. Setting short-term goals that keep us grounded while remaining open to adjustments along the way can also help.
- **Acceptance**: Embracing change involves accepting the uncertainty it brings and acknowledging that it's okay not to have all the answers. This allows you to approach transitions with a sense of curiosity and openness to discovery.

CONTINUED SUPPORT

As much as change is a personal journey, you never have to face it alone. Seeking support during times of significant change not only provides a safety net but also enriches your journey with shared wisdom and encouragement that you will acquire. Equipping yourself with the right tools and support can make all the difference in turning your vision into reality. Connect with people who embody the qualities you admire or has achieved similar goals.

- **Community**: Whether it's friends, family, or a support group, surrounding yourself with a compassionate community offers practical assistance and emotional sustenance. It creates a space for shared experiences and a place where understanding can flourish.
- **Professional guidance**: Sometimes, the insight of professionals, such as counselors or life coaches can help you in navigating change. Their expertise can offer new perspectives on your situation and provide tools and strategies to manage transitions more effectively.
- **Mentorship**: A mentor can offer invaluable guidance, encouragement, and insights from their journey. Connecting with someone who has navigated similar changes can provide both inspiration and practical advice that can be used as a roadmap and help to avoid pitfalls along the way.

In navigating new relationships with confidence and clarity, we draw upon what we have learned, our self-understanding, communication skills, intuitive awareness, and the gratitude we have nurtured. These tools guide us in forming meaningful connections and enrich our journey. As we move forward, let us embrace these principles, allowing them to shape our interactions with others and enhance the bonds we form.

MAINTAINING CURIOSITY, SELF-DISCOVERY AND GROWTH

Curiosity is the driving force behind exploration and discovery and keeps the journey of self-discovery vibrant and exciting. It encourages you to ask questions, to look beyond the surface, and to seek the 'why' and 'how.' This relentless inquiry broadens your understanding of the world and deepens your connection with yourself. Cultivate your curiosity by doing this:

- **Ask questions**: Cultivate a habit of questioning. Every question asked is a step towards greater understanding, from the mundane to the monumental. Show that you are truly curious and want to learn so that your questioning is appreciated and reflects the value of it.
- **Embrace the unknown**: The unknown is not to be feared but embraced. It holds endless possibilities for learning and growth.

In the realm of personal development, the pursuit of knowledge and understanding about yourself never really ends. This ongoing quest is not a series of steps to be checked off. It enriches every aspect of your life with depth and meaning. You are discovering new facets of being and integrating these insights into the core of who you truly are.

The appetite for learning is a flame that should be nurtured throughout life. It fuels your progress, pushing you to question, explore, and expand your horizons. This quest for knowledge transcends traditional academic pursuits and encompasses everything from mastering new skills to exploring unfamiliar cultures and ideologies. It challenges your preconceptions, encourages adaptability, and fosters a resilient, open mind that thrives on diversity and change. Here are a few ways to keep the flame of learning alive:

- **Explore varied interests**: Permit yourself to pursue a range of subjects, even those outside your comfort zone. Each new area of knowledge brings a fresh perspective and a greater understanding of the world and your place within it.
- **Seek challenges**: Challenges are not just obstacles but opportunities to stretch your capabilities and discover new strengths. Whether learning a new language or tackling a complex problem, overcoming each challenge adds another layer to your self-knowledge and gives you more insight and confidence.

BOUNDARY SETTING: A LIFELONG PRACTICE

Boundaries are like the roots of a tree; they anchor us, allowing for growth in various directions while keeping us connected to what is vital. Over time, as the tree matures, these roots might shift, expand, or deepen. Similarly, our personal boundaries evolve as we navigate life's different stages and milestones. Recognizing this intrinsic nature is critical to maintaining a healthy balance and always protecting our well-being. Life doesn't stand still. Our needs, desires, and circumstances change as we move through it.

Your boundaries will change throughout the years. For instance, the early years might focus on career ambitions, requiring boundaries around work-life balance. Later, the focus might shift towards family or personal fulfillment, necessitating adjustments in allocating your time and energy. This evolution is natural and reflects your growth as an individual. It is wise to periodically assess and adjust your boundaries to reflect your current life phase and priorities. Allow yourself the flexibility to modify your boundaries as necessary. Rigidity causes stress and resentment, counteracting the very purpose of setting limits in the first place.

Life throws curveballs, and we might find ourselves in situations that test the limits of our established boundaries. A typical scenario is family dynamics, such as an adult child needing to move back home. In an instance like this, clarity and communication are paramount. Before the move, have a candid conversation about expectations, responsibilities, and a timeline for the arrangement. This preemptive approach helps minimize potential conflict and ensures that everyone's needs are considered. Boundaries empower us to establish patterns of interaction that are respectful, fulfilling, and nurturing.

- **Communicate:** Specifying your exact needs is imperative to avoid assumptions. Clearly state them to minimize any misunderstandings and to provide the foundation for the dynamics of interactions.
- **Stay consistent**: When people know you're firm with your limits, they're more likely to respect them. If faced with resistance, don't give in.
- **Reiterate**: Remind those around you the importance of boundaries for both mutual respect and

understanding each other's needs. Every time you enforce a boundary, you reaffirm your worth.

At the core of boundary setting is the act of self-respect. It is a declaration that your needs, time, and well-being are valuable. In a world that often pressures us to prioritize others, asserting our boundaries can sometimes be misunderstood as selfishness. However, this is far from the truth. By safeguarding your mental and emotional health, you are enhancing your ability to engage more fully and authentically with the world. Boundaries help cultivate relationships that are supportive, respectful, and enriching.

Having boundaries set in place allows you to nurture your capacity to participate in relationships and activities in a healthy, balanced manner. Remember, caring for your needs benefits you and the people you interact with. Being well-rested and happy allows you to be more attentive and capable of showing compassion, empathy, and support. By staying aware of the significance of your boundaries, you honor your needs, respect yourself enough to uphold these limits, and create an environment where your well-being is prioritized. This ongoing act of self-respect strengthens your sense of self and allows you to have a better connection with others.

The path of self-discovery and growth is uniquely yours. It's a road marked by continuous learning, change, and reflection, anchoring your experiences into your psyche. Each step on this path enriches your understanding and amplifies your capacity to live fully and authentically with a curiosity about the world and yourself. As you transform from this exploration, understand that growth and learning are not destinations but processes that help you see what you might not have seen, open doors you might not have noticed, and enrich your life with wisdom and wonder.

If you run into a wall, don't turn around and give up. Figure out how to climb it.

— MICHAEL JORDAN

MOVING FORWARD WITH YOUR LIFE

Let yourself be silently drawn by the strange pull of what you really love. It will not lead you astray.

— RUMI

Moving forward from a toxic relationship marks a courageous step toward regaining freedom and emotional well-being and letting go of the remaining hurtful remnants. There is a continuous, ongoing reclamation of your sense of identity with the pursuit of your passions and aspirations. This renewed embracing of life requires a balance between self-growth and self-care, and as you do this, you vastly increase your understanding of your self-worth.

In this journey of personal growth, it is necessary to find the balance between self-care and self-challenge. These two elements go hand in hand and support each other. Self-care and self-challenge are not opposing teams but are like complementary colors in the palette of your life. One nurtures and replenishes, while the other propels you into unexplored realms. Each holds its weight, pulling you toward a center where growth and well-being coexist. This equilibrium is delicate, a gentle tug-of-war between comfort and courage, rest and adventure. It beckons you to step into the unknown while ensuring the foundation beneath you is solid and nurturing. Finding this requires some effort, but within this precarious dance, you discover your true potential.

Growth resides in stepping out of your comfort zone and the willingness to stretch beyond familiar boundaries.

Challenging yourself is an act of courage, a deliberate step into the unknown for personal expansion. Whether it's learning a new skill, pursuing a long-held dream, or simply changing an ingrained habit, these challenges push you to new heights. Remember, stepping out of your comfort zone is about stretching yourself, discovering new possibilities, and realizing your full potential. It may feel uncomfortable at first, but the rewards of personal growth and self-discovery are well worth it.

- **Set personal challenges**: Identify areas of your life you wish to improve or goals you aspire to achieve. Break these down into tangible, achievable challenges that push your limits.
- **Overcome fears**: Fear often stands between you and your potential. Although fear was designed to keep you safe, it is also what holds you back. Face your fears head-on, understanding that fear is not a sign to retreat but to proceed with caution and courage.

Physical activity and emotional wellness are intertwined, influencing and supporting each other. The care you extend to your body echoes into your emotional spaces, increasing your capacity for resilience and healing. Physical health becomes vital for growing and flourishing and supporting this balance. Certain yoga poses require you to support your body weight, which builds muscle strength, particularly in your core, arms, legs, and back but also challenge yourself by using free weights. Strength training builds your confidence as you physically become stronger.

Working out with dumbbells and building muscle has multiple advantages, not only with increased muscle strength but also with your endurance, agility, and coordination, making daily activities easier to do. In addition, strength training reduces anxiety and depression, improves your mood, and increases your self-esteem. Each weight lifted, each muscle stretched, represents your capacity to endure and overcome. Working out with weights teaches discipline, resilience, and the importance of pushing beyond comfort to achieve growth. It's a physical manifestation of your inner strength and a reminder that you can face and surmount the obstacles before you.

- **Start small**: Begin with exercises that match your current fitness level, gradually increasing intensity as your strength improves.
- **Focus on your strengths**. Don't compare yourself to others. Accept and appreciate your body and realize that you are a unique individual.
- **Maintain Self-compassion**: Always remember to find the balance between self-challenge and self-care.

If you are ever pushing yourself too hard, stop and check to see if an unworthy belief has resurfaced. With this awareness, release any negative self-talk with compassion.
- **Be Consistent**: Regular strength training contributes to physical and mental health enabling you to comfortably face challenges head-on.

LISTENING TO BOTH YOUR INNER NEEDS AND INTUITION

Amidst the push and pull of self-care and self-challenge lies a deeper calling to truly listen to your inner needs. This internal dialogue guides you, offering clues on when to press forward and when to pull back. Ignoring this voice can lead to burnout while heeding its wisdom fosters a sustainable path to growth.

- **Check-in regularly**: Make it a practice to check in with yourself, assessing your mental, emotional, and physical state. This regular practice helps you adjust your balance of self-care and self-challenge as needed.
- **Silence the inner critic**: The voice that doubts and criticizes can drown out your true needs. Cultivate a practice of self-compassion, speaking to yourself with kindness and understanding, especially in moments of challenge or uncertainty.

Trust your intuition. It is your internal compass, offering subtle cues and insights often overlooked by the rational mind. The more you develop it, the easier it becomes to connect with it. In new relationships, this gut feeling can guide you towards connections that resonate with your true self and steer you away from those that do not align with your path.

- **Tune in to your feelings**: Pay attention to how you feel around new acquaintances. Do they uplift you, or do they drain you? Your emotional responses can provide valuable guidance.
- **Permit yourself to step back**: It's okay to pause and reassess if something feels off. Trusting your intuition means honoring those internal signals, even if they lead you away from a budding connection.

Creativity flows through every aspect of existence, from the morning dew on a spider's web to the intricate patterns of human thought.

Creativity is the silent language of the soul, offering a bridge between the internal world of emotions and the external realm of expression. Engaging in creative activities isn't just a pastime; it's a vital process of self-discovery and healing. It helps free you from the control of a toxic relationship.

The spectrum of creativity is vast, encompassing more than just the traditional arts. It finds expression in cooking, gardening, writing, and even how we solve daily problems. To tap into this wellspring of innovation, start by exploring activities that pique your curiosity or reignite a long-forgotten passion. Whether picking up a paintbrush, strumming a guitar, or writing a poem, each act of creation is a step toward understanding and articulating your inner experiences and expressing who you are. Consider these activities:

- **Photography**: Capturing moments through a camera lens can help you see the world from new perspectives, notice beauty in the mundane, and appreciate things more.
- **Dance**: Movement to music is a physical release and a way to express emotions non-verbally.
- **Crafting**: Activities like knitting, woodworking, pottery, and sewing all require focus and patience, providing a meditative escape and a tangible sense of accomplishment.

OVERCOMING CREATIVE BLOCKS AND SHARING YOUR CREATIVE WORKS

It's not uncommon to encounter obstacles in your creative journey. These blocks, whether stemming from fear, self-doubt, or external pressures, can stifle your creative expression. Overcoming them requires patience, self-compassion, and a few strategic approaches:

- **Start simple**: There are many adult coloring books that provide inspirational thoughts. Buy crayons or colored pencils and start drawing and illustrating simple things that make you happy.
- **Routine**: Set aside regular time for creative activities, treating them as non-negotiable parts of your day. Consistency can help break through blocks over time.
- **Permission to be imperfect**: Allow yourself to create without judgment. Remember, the value lies in the process, not just the outcome.

- **Inspiration**: Seek out new experiences, ideas, and environments. Sometimes, a change of scenery or a fresh perspective can ignite creative sparks.

Sharing your creations with others can be both exhilarating and intimidating. It takes a leap of faith and a willingness to be vulnerable. This vulnerability holds the strength and the potential to inspire and connect deeply with others. Here are some avenues for sharing:

- **Social media**: Platforms like Instagram or Pinterest are great places to showcase your work and connect with a community of like-minded individuals.
- **Blogs and websites**: Creating a personal blog or website can serve as a digital portfolio, offering a space to share your journey and creations with a broader audience.
- **Local exhibits and performances**: Participating in local art shows, open mic nights, or craft fairs can provide real-world opportunities to share your work, receive feedback, and meet new people.

As you explore your creative side, embrace this as a tool for healing. As you overcome blocks and share your work with the world, your inner journey unfolds in colors, words, and movements. This process enriches your personal growth. Your creativity captures the essence of your journey and can encourage others to embrace the healing benefits of being creative.

SELF-KNOWLEDGE IS THE FOUNDATION FOR HEALTHY RELATIONSHIPS

Before entering into a new relationship, use the self-knowledge you have obtained to help guide you with assurance and poise. This deep understanding of your values, needs, and boundaries allows you to safely engage with others and approach relationships from a place of authenticity.

- **Reflect on past interactions**: Consider what has and hasn't worked for you in previous relationships. Use these reflections to identify patterns that can inform your approach to new connections.
- **Acknowledge your worth**: Recognize that your value does not fluctuate based on others' perceptions. This steadfast belief in yourself is attractive and sets a precedent for how others treat you.

Clear, honest communication is the cornerstone of any healthy relationship, allowing for the exchange of ideas, feelings, and expectations. At the heart of fostering new connections lies the opportunity for fulfilling and enriching experiences. In new relationships, establishing clarity from the start can prevent misunderstandings and build a strong foundation for future interactions.

- **Express your needs and desires**: Don't hesitate to communicate your expectations and limits. Being upfront about what you seek in a relationship fosters mutual respect and understanding.

- **Practice active listening**: Communication is a two-way street. Show the same level of openness and attentiveness you desire, creating a space where both parties feel heard and valued.

ENVISIONING AND BUILDING A NEW LEGACY

No matter your age, creating a legacy shows that you truly value yourself and your accomplishments Taking a mindful approach to living ensures that your legacy is created by the conscious choices you make, filled with the wisdom and compassion you have gained. This vision of a healthier legacy becomes your blueprint, guiding your choices and interactions. It serves as a reminder that every step taken in healing builds the foundation of a new legacy you can be proud of.

- **Daily reflection**: Dedicate time each day to reflect on your actions and decisions. What values do you wish to pass along? Are they aligned with the legacy you wish to create?
- **Define your core values**: Pinpoint the principles that you hold dear and wish to be remembered by. Is it the courage to stand up for yourself, the importance of self-care, or the strength found in vulnerability?
- **Live by example**: Embody these values in your daily life. Your actions serve as the most potent testament to the legacy you are building.
- **Mindful interactions**: Approach each interaction with presence and empathy. This mindful

engagement with others seeds the values of your legacy in the present time.

CREATING AN IMPACT AND EMPOWERING OTHERS THROUGH YOUR STORY

Sharing both the obstacles and the unexpected help you received along your journey of regaining your true self can light the way for others. It is a gesture that says, "If I could navigate through the storm, so can you." There is strength within every story of resilience and the impact it has, not just on individuals but across generations. Recognizing that each of us holds the potential to be the catalyst for change, to end cycles of negativity within our families, communities, and beyond is powerful.

In stepping forward to share your story, you take on the role of a leader, illustrating that it is possible to move beyond past traumas to forge healthier patterns of living and relating. This becomes a powerful declaration that the chains of unhealthy relationships can be broken and that a new, vibrant lineage of emotional strength and resilience can be established. Your struggles and triumphs carry the seeds of empowerment for others. Your resilience demonstrates the courage to rise each time you face a challenge.

The impact of sharing your story extends far beyond the immediate moment of connection. Choose platforms or mediums that feel safe and supportive, whether through writing, speaking engagements, or one-on-one conversations. Focus on your growth. Highlight the lessons you have learned and the progress you made through your challenges. This has the potential to touch lives in ways you might never fully know, sparking courage and fostering healing in others. This sharing becomes a significant component of your healing process, reaffirming your journey and the strength you've gathered along the way.

Consider mentoring others who are navigating similar paths. Your insights and encouragement can be invaluable to someone just beginning their journey. Become involved with the community. Engage with community projects or initiatives that resonate with your values. Your involvement amplifies your healing and growth, elevating your confidence and impacting your community even more.

The stories you share, the values you embody, and the mindful approaches you adopt all contribute to the legacy of how much you have grown. Your strength, resilience, and compassion are a testament to your journey and a hope for future generations. It underscores the profound truth that healing is not just a personal endeavor but a gift that, when shared, can transform lives, and reshape destinies.

As you move forward, do so with the intention of nurturing your growth and encouraging and empowering others around you. By openly sharing your narrative, you offer proof that it's possible to emerge stronger and more compassionate from harsh adversity. Your resilience inspires others to confront their challenges with renewed hope and determination to live their lives to their fullest potential. This is the essence of knowing and embracing your true worth.

Strength does not come from physical capacity. It comes from an indomitable will.

— MAHATMA GANDHI

CONCLUSION

Being in a toxic relationship does not define who you are. Your capacity for love and fulfillment exists and can always grow and thrive. You have taken the steps to break free, heal, and rebuild a life that aligns with your truth. You have learned to recognize the harm of toxic relationships, walk away from them, and learned ways to love and value yourself. By doing this, you have made substantial progress in your soul's journey.

This journey takes time and requires strength, courage, and continuous self-care. It's crucial to always treat yourself with kindness and to celebrate each step forward. The part of your life that was marked by pain and confusion has now brought you to a place of empowerment, self-love, and awareness. Wherever you are on this path, feel a sense of gratitude for the transformation that has transpired because of your continuous efforts. It has become a testament to your resilience and determination. Celebrate your accomplishments because they reflect your inner power.

Going through this experience, while very unpleasant, revealed the truth that the power of transformation lies within you. Self-compassion and patience are vital in the recovery process. The path to healing and growth is not a straight line. It twists, turns abruptly and sometimes takes unexpected leaps. The process of rebuilding is not a race but a slow unfolding of steps that leads to discovering your true self.

I encourage you to continue your path of creating a better life, one filled with confidence, joy and empowerment. Embrace lifelong learning with eagerness and view each challenge as an opportunity to grow. Let your life be a transparent picture of your core values and aspirations. Remember, you are not alone on this journey. Community and support are crucial in your path to healing. The bonds you form with friends and family who genuinely care for you hold immense strength. Reach out, share your burden, and extend your hand to others. In giving support, you receive it tenfold, reinforcing the idea that no one is ever truly alone in their struggles.

Please keep this message of hope and resilience going:

> *You possess the strength to emerge from a toxic relationship stronger, more self-aware, and empowered to cultivate healthy, loving relationships with yourself and others around you.*

Walk with your head held high, knowing that with each step forward, you demonstrate your confidence and faith in your ability to create a life filled with hope, love, and endless possibilities.

In conclusion, I invite you to share your story. Your narrative of overcoming painful times can inspire hope in the hearts of those who may still be trapped in fear and doubt. Your experiences can help others feel understood and less isolated. You can create a ripple effect of empowerment and the beginning of a new cycle of healing in other individuals who need the courage to walk away from a toxic relationship and to embrace a life of trust, love and self-respect.

I believe in being strong when everything seems to be going wrong. I believe that happy girls are the prettiest girls. I believe tomorrow is another day and I believe in miracles.

— AUDREY HEPBURN

MAKE A DIFFERENCE WITH A REVIEW

Be the change you want to see in the world.

— MAHATMA GANDHI

If you could help someone else, someone in need, someone you never met, would you?

You can help that individual by leaving a review for this book.

Genuine compassion lies in the ability to understand the silent battles of others, especially those fighting to love themselves in a world that constantly tells them they're not enough.

Would you help someone you've never met, even if you never got credit for it?

Who is this person, you ask? They are like you—or, at least, like you used to be—less experienced, wanting a change and needing help but not sure where to look.

My goal is to make "Letting Go of Toxic Relationships" help as many people as possible. And, the only way to accomplish that is by reaching everyone who needs this help.

This is where you come in. Most people do, in fact, judge a book by its cover as well as its reviews. So, on behalf of a struggling reader you've never met, please write a review.

This is a gift that costs only a minute of your time, and it can change a fellow reader's life forever. Your review can help...

...one more person break free from toxic patterns.
...one more individual find inner peace.
...one more soul embrace self-love.
...one more heart heal from past wounds.

Simply scan the QR code below to leave your review:

If you feel good about helping someone you never met, you are a beautiful soul. You are one of the compassionate ones.

Thank you for considering leaving a review. Your support means the world to me and to those who will benefit from this book.

REFERENCES

Setting Healthy Boundaries in Relationships - HelpGuide.org https://www.helpguide.org/articles/relationships-communication/setting-healthy-boundaries-in-relationships.htm

What are the Short and Long-Term Effects of Emotional Abuse https://www.healthline.com/health/mental-health/effects-of-emotional-abuse

Understanding the Impact of Childhood Trauma on Adult Relationships https://www.masterscounselling.com/s/stories/understanding-the-impact-of-childhood-trauma-on-adult-relationships

Victim Mentality: Causes, Symptoms, and More - WebMD https://www.webmd.com/mental-health/what-is-a-victim-mentality

Attachment Styles and How They Affect Adult Relationships https://www.helpguide.org/articles/relationships-communication/attachment-and-adult-relationships.htm

8 Ways to Start Healing Your Inner Child - Healthline https://www.healthline.com/health/mental-health/inner-child-healing

Transcending childhood trauma in adult relationships https://www.counselling-directory.org.uk/memberarticles/transcending-childhood-trauma-in-adult-relationships

Mindfulness exercises - Mayo Clinic https://www.mayoclinic.org/healthy-lifestyle/consumer-health/in-depth/mindfulness-exercises/art-20046356

Achieving Personal Empowerment - Taking Charge of Your Life and Career https://www.mindtools.com/aiaydss/achieving-personal-empowerment

The Importance of Support Groups in Recovery https://www.thecabinsydney.com.au/blog/the-importance-of-support-groups-in-recovery/

How to Set Boundaries with Your Family https://time.com/6331383/how-to-set-boundaries-family/

Rebuilding Your Finances After Financial Abuse https://www.bankrate.com/personal-finance/rebuild-finances-after-financial-abuse/

How Childhood Trauma May Affect Adult Relationships https://psychcentral.com/blog/how-childhood-trauma-affects-adult-relationships

Setting Healthy Boundaries in Relationships https://www.helpguide.org/

articles/relationships-communication/setting-healthy-boundaries-in-relationships.htm

Role of Physical Activity on Mental Health and Well-Being https://www.ncbi.nlm.nih.gov/pmc/articles/PMC9902068/